A PERSONAL TESTIMONY

Lessons On What the Shepherd Does for the Sheep

H. Bernard Young Sr.

A Personal Testimony
Lessons On What the Shepherd Does for the Sheep
Copyright © 2020 by H. Bernard Young Sr.

Library of Congress Control Number:		2019916159
ISBN-13:	Paperback:	978-1-64674-039-0
	PDF:	978-1-64674-040-6
	ePub:	978-1-64674-041-3
	Kindle:	978-1-64674-042-0

Printed in the United States of America

LitFire
PUBLISHING

LitFire LLC
1-800-511-9787
www.litfirepublishing.com
order@litfirepublishing.com

Contents

FOREWORD

The interaction between a shepherd and sheep is one of nature's most intriguing relational concepts. This ancient social exchange serves as a practical illustration of the believer's personal bond with the Lord himself. Undoubtedly, Psalm 23 captures this spiritual reality unlike any other literary source known to mankind.

This psalm highlights David's personal encounter with the Lord and expresses the unlimited benefits of being in the sovereign care of a loving shepherd. It serves as a scriptural model of the wonderful possibilities God offers those who trust Him as their shepherd. Like David, all humanity stands in need of the Shepherd and His overwhelming love for His sheep.

The severity of this powerful truth motivated my friend, H. Bernard Young, to write this powerful spiritual resource that you are about to experience. A personal testimony offers timeless truth from the Word of God that will introduce or draw you closer to the Lord.

The pages ahead offer a refreshing, in-depth, and practical resource that will enhance our understanding of our current or potential relationship with the Lord. I pray that this book serves as a spiritual compass to those who desire an intimate relationship with God, our Shepherd.

Pastor Paul Little, II

To my parents, Mr. and Mrs. Herbert Young Jr., for giving me what a godly example should look like; to my sister who supports me continually; and to my wife, Dolores, who has been by my side; and my children, Kerek, Bernautica, Bianca, and BJ; and my precious G-baby, Journee.

To my Thankful Church family, I love you and thank you for your continued support. I thank God for allowing me the revered opportunity to serve as your pastor.

H. BERNARD YOUNG SR.

INTRODUCTION

One of the most lyrical theological masterpieces ever written was recorded in Psalm 23. It is composed by one who is, in fact, a musician himself. This lyrical dynamic deals with personal relationship, provision, protection, peril, and promises. When we look at the lyrics of this psalm, it gives testimony of a powerful relationship one has when they are in the Shepherd's care.

Yes, the Shepherd is mentioned in the lyrics of this psalm in an intimate, close, and personal way. The psalmist mentions Him in the very beginning of this psalm and honors Him to the fullest extent and praises Him in the totality of His glory. What such fitting lyrics this psalm contains as it certainly blesses all generations. The lyrics of this psalm deals with relationship, honor, and benefits.

This psalm is not only a lyrical masterpiece, it is expressed with metaphorical language that explains the Shepherd in the life of the sheep. The psalmist has a purpose for praising God because he realizes the presence and power of God in many ways. Therefore, he begins to testify about God's shepherding provision, peace, protection, and power as he experiences these benefits. He experiences and appreciates the Shepherd's guidance.

Guidance is needed when you have no idea as to what you must do and where you must go. In fact, you have no resolve to any situation because you wonder in spiritual un-fulfillment that's leaving you directionless. You are at a place of spiritual confusion because you have no guidance nor direction. You cannot comprehend nor discern what's important for you simply because you have no directional guidance on what to do or where you should be. Therefore, due to your unfulfilled state, you are discombobulated because you have a void, you possess an emptiness, you are missing something significant, and your absence of spiritual guidance shows tremendously.

Your spiritual deficiency proves undoubtedly that you need the Shepherd. You need to develop a relationship. The relationship basis is on a level of leader and follower. A relationship of guidance. In fact, due to your lack of guidance, you don't know how to trust because you are a stranger to having spiritual guidance and spiritual submission. In addition, this confirms that you are indeed without the Shepherd and need Him in your life due to relationship deficiency.

Having a relationship with God is imperative. When we possess a relationship with God, it displays a distinction between God and the believer. The believer has an awesome responsibility to come to a place in their spiritual life to get in contact with God and remain connected to Him. Experiencing the Christian life is not easy and there are many challenges we face during our relationship with God.

Therefore, when we face consistent challenges and conflicting circumstances, we find ourselves at a place of proving our trust in God. Furthermore, when we face our circumstances head on, it, without a doubt, proves who we are as believers and disciples of Christ. Moreover, when a disciple goes through strenuous times, they should know their spiritual identity and status. We should know by now we are not on the same level as God; we are inferior, He is superior. In fact, the reason why we are called inferior is that we are called, from a Biblical perspective, sheep. In like manner, from a Biblical perspective, the superior is God, the Shepherd.

Subsequently, this psalm deals with an individual (sheep) who have had encounters with God and sees how God (shepherd) takes care of His sheep and provides the necessities for his journey of peace, prosperity, and protection. This sheep has a name meaning beloved; he spent his years of youth in Bethlehem; he was the youngest of eight brothers; the son of Jessie; his mother was honored for her godliness; he was, by occupation, a keeper of sheep; he was also an awesome anointed musician.

This individual has pronounced himself as sheep and God as the shepherd. He has had multiple experiences, challenges, and circumstances in life to have a total understanding of what the Shepherd is to the sheep. Therefore, as he witnesses the totality of God's grace and guidance, he then understands not only what He is to the sheep, but he now understands what the Shepherd does for the sheep.

A shepherd is what's needed when sheep go astray, need nurturing, lack discipline, commitment, and have a lack of nourishment. The sheep have no guidance, no direction, no forerunner, no leader, no encourager, no protector, no provider, no peacemaker. Therefore, shepherding is essential to sheep because sheep need directional leadership.

Needing a good shepherd for leadership is important to the lifetime supply of the sheep. In fact, when it seems like provision is absent, prosperity is lacking, and peace is missing, it confuses one into thinking, *Does God really care about me?* Shepherding is not a lost calling. Actually, this calling takes place in the Old Testament; in Ancient Israel the people were considered pastoral people. There were also Biblical patriarchs who were labeled as shepherds, such as Abraham, Jacob, Moses, King David, and Amos were natural shepherds. The Old Testament gives reference to shepherding (Psalm 80:1) and (Ezekiel 34:14) where God is viewed as Israel's servant leader. In addition, the New Testament reveals shepherding from a New Covenant perspective (John 10:11). Furthermore, shepherding has always taken place in the scriptures.

One thing for sure, sheep need a shepherd. They need someone who can lead them to the designated places and direct their paths. They need direction, love, compassion, mercy, discipline, purpose, protection, and guidance. When sheep have no shepherd (guidance) they are vulnerable and subject to do anything. In nature, sheep catch anxiety when they have no social contact because they are sociable animals. So then, if sheep have no shepherd, they have no purposeful directional leadership nor sense of security nor any fellowship.

Have you ever pondered in your mind, *Does God really care about me?* Yes, He cares about you. In my opinion, Psalm 23 is one of the most inspiring writings in all the Psalms and perhaps all of scripture. This sacred literature is valued by believers. Many believers say that this is one of their favorite psalms. Some also suggest this is their favorite of all scripture. This Psalm is an awesome way to understand how God loves His children, delivers His children and shows them that He is their Shepherd and will give them whatever they need and take care of them.

This Psalm is one of the most quoted Psalms. In fact, it is mentioned at funerals and other church gatherings. It is one of the most popular scriptures perhaps in all the Bible. This psalm is on many marketing products and etc. Actually, this psalm is read at weddings and funerals. However, in reference to funerals, this psalm is not for the dead; it is for the living. In other gatherings or church functions, this psalm is quoted often. The psalmist writes in this lyrical composition just how the Shepherd makes a way for His sheep. This particular psalm is peculiar because, if noticed carefully, the Shepherd (God) is silent and the sheep (David) does the speaking. He clarifies in this exquisite song, in fact, how the Shepherd cares for His sheep by expressing his personal testimony.

Understanding Sheep

Understanding the sheep could be a complex thing but yet simple. We know sheep need a shepherd because they have no guidance, and therefore, the shepherd is there to guide the sheep and protect them. Additionally speaking, sheep have intellectual issues that cause them not to be intelligent but have amazing instincts. No one understands sheep like the shepherd or, like in modern-day terms, the handler of sheep.

This particular individual (which is David) who wrote this psalm is praised for this psalm in multiple ways. Psalm 23 is valued highly by the Christian community. However, the reality is the author of this psalm has not always given his attention totally to God. Therefore, this psalm is valued highly by others. However, the person who wrote the psalm did not always have a God-like past.

The psalmist had some issues before he faithfully wrote the beloved Psalm 23. The psalmist had some issues and one of his difficulties was with his flesh. He was infatuated with women, and one day, he saw Bathsheba bathing. He was captivated by the beauty of her physical presence and eventually laid with her. As a result, she became pregnant and when David discovers he's the father, he tries to cover up his sin. He has Uriah to come home from battle, but he would not fulfill David's plan. He wouldn't sleep with his wife, Bathsheba. This infuriated David and he ordered and caused the death of her husband by sending him to war. In fact, David did some things that were not pleasing in the very sight of God. However, he still possessed the favor of God.

Eventually, David becomes a man after God's own heart and strives to please God totally. Therefore, David knows in fact what God can do for an individual on a personal and spiritual level. Furthermore, as God dealt with David and changed his life, so can He do for us, and we will know what a shepherd does for His sheep and we can testify to others the goodness of God.

Within our humanity, we have setbacks and have done things we are not proud of, but the saving grace of our God supplies our needs and provides great shepherding care for the sheep.

Psalm 23 is a masterpiece of the greatness of our God and how He functions to give His sheep what they need. There have been many challenges we faced, difficulties, setbacks, trials, tribulations, turbulent test, and even tragedies. We experience multiple storms in life; therefore, while encountering the storms, God gives us specific things that give us the sustaining grace to survive the very oppressive and tough moments life distributes to us, disturbing the atmosphere. Life is certainly not easy. There are consistent conflicts that come our way. But God somehow comes to our rescue and demonstrates His everlasting compassion and grace toward us.

The struggles life gives sometimes are very strenuous and stressful, and sometimes causes one to surrender to life's strongholds. However, with the help of the Shepherd, sheep can survive the challenges of life and go to the places the Shepherd can lead them to. There are many times we feel as though we will not make it during the painful processes of our lives, but the Shepherd is there. Although, the painful moments we encounter are for our development, not our detriment.

Sheep by Nature

By nature, sheep have a strong instinct to follow other sheep that are in front of them. In fact, every flock has a leader. Sheep will follow the sheep in front of them, and sometimes, the herd leader will lead other sheep into unsafe places. Sometimes they may even go to the edge of a cliff, and if the sheep are following them, they will most likely fall over the cliff as well, because by nature, sheep follow the sheep that are ahead of them. Some sheep have even died because of following the sheep that lead, not realizing they could be led into danger because, by nature, sheep follow.

In fact, even from birth, lambs are fashioned to follow the elder members of the flock because, by nature, that's what they do—they are followers.

However, even though they are followers, some sheep still get ahead of the flock and other sheep will follow them wherever they go. It is very dangerous to follow someone or something that has no idea of where they are going. They have no idea of where they are going because they have distorted vision. Due to them not having the gift of leadership, they are vulnerable and subject to be led anywhere because, by nature, they were designed to follow and not lead.

What causes sheep to flock together is somewhat beneficial because they arc very social animals. In fact, according to animal behaviorists, "Sheep most of the time will graze with at least four or five sheep." They are social because they like a visual connection to other sheep and they mostly like to stay in numbers. Sheep stay in numbers because they feel safe with other sheep, feeling the sense of community. However, the sad reality is they can still end up in a bad environment due to not having a shepherd.

Another fact about sheep is they flee from fights. Sheep are not predators, they are prey. They will try to avoid any act of violence because their instinct is to flee from any sense of trouble. Sheep also have a very high tolerance level for pain. They naturally won't show their pain because if they did, it would show that they are in fact even more vulnerable. In addition, sheep are classified as healthy or unhealthy based on their appetite. One of the indicators of healthy sheep is they always have an appetite to eat. Sheep which are healthy normally eat and chew on their cud for multiple hours daily. Healthy sheep have consistent hunger and will overeat if their shepherd allows them to do so. In contrast, sheep that contain a lack of appetite are normally diagnosed as sick sheep. When sheep are sick or in pain, it normally reacts differently than healthy sheep. For instance, if sheep are sick they mostly at times are hesitant to get up from rest because of pain. Also, when sheep are in pain, it takes them a long time to lay down and rest. Another sign of pain for sheep is when they grind their teeth.

I've had a deep interest in this particular psalm for a long time. In fact, I wanted to know more about sheep in a very significant and distinct way. I wanted to know how sheep operate and function from a natural context. Instead of having a mental assumption and picture of how sheep functioned, I wanted a hands-on experience. I mentally saw this psalm in a certain way before I understood how sheep actually function. After having this craving for understanding sheep from an actual perspective as opposed to an assuming perspective, I contacted a sheep farm and I made an appointment with a shepherdess. As I traveled, I went to a sheep farm in central Georgia, and as I drove by, there they were—sheep!

I was extremely excited about going to this sheep farm because I wanted to know and understand sheep in totality, naturally, socially, and their behavior patterns. As I met the shepherdess, she began to share vital information about sheep and the shared information actually blew my mind. While she was talking, I was in awe; I was like a listener eager to hear good news. I was like an interested parishioner and serious disciple wanting to hear an awesome sermon by its pastor. She had me hook, line, and sinker. I bought into what she was selling. As I sat, I was like a sponge and I absorbed all the information I could.

The experience I had on this sheep farm made things more enlightening and understandable. While the shepherdess educated me on the social actions and behavioral patterns of sheep, I was fascinated, then, it dawned on me: now I understand why sheep need a shepherd for leadership. The lessons she gave me about sheep were priceless and her teaching is something I will treasure forever. In addition, this additional information I received about sheep gave me another way to look at sheep by nature.

While listening to the shepherdess' lesson concerning the nature, social skills, and behavior patterns of sheep, I clearly saw the spiritual principles behind the relationship between the shepherd and sheep. The simple things I learned on the sheep farm from a perspective of nature made sense to apply spiritually in order to have the illumination of not only Psalm23, but the bond the Shepherd (God) and sheep (people) share. The lessons of the interview with the shepherdess reminded me of my calling as an under-shepherd. The basic things about sheep naturally confirm just who sheep are from a relationship perspective. The shepherdess shared with me the following about sheep: (1) they depend on their shepherd; (2) they are subordinate to their shepherd; (3) they submit to their shepherd; (4) they know the voice of their shepherd. These very basic principles I learned about sheep in reference to nature have very powerful implications from a perspective of spirituality.

Spiritually speaking, we are considered as sheep and we depend on the Shepherd because we know we cannot survive or be sustained without His presence in our lives: we know who's at the top of the realm. It's not sheep, it's the Shepherd. He's over all things; we are to submit to Him in our personal lives and also in the life of the church if we desire to be used authentically and effectively by Him; and we actually know His voice (John 10:27).

To that end, there are sheep and they are in two categories: there are healthy sheep and unhealthy sheep. Since I've concisely stated some natural things about sheep, let's now focus our attention on one of the most beloved scriptures in all the Bible and that is Psalm 23. David begins this psalm awesomely and authentically. I admire the way David starts this psalm; he begins this psalm with the Lord.

The Lord

Psalm 23 gives irrefutable evidence of how God always provides when we are in a position of lack. Honestly, there are many things we lack, but God makes up the difference because He is our Lord and He's all sufficient. This is a great way to begin this psalm, with the Lord.

The Psalmist suggests that the Lord is his shepherd. The Lord *yehōwāh* which means God. His name means existence, availability, capability, and power. In Exodus 3:14, it is simply put, "I AM THAT I AM," God is all-sufficient and all-powerful; therefore, He has the power and authority to bless His children and preserve them from persistent danger and consistently bless them with His blessings and provide what we need.

What the Exodus account explains to us is that God is more than enough to meet our needs and exceed them. We have a God that has the power to give us exactly what we need and more. When we think about the sufficiency of God, what should come to mind? "I AM" being the personal name of Israel's God. His name literally means "to be." This means that He can be the solution to all our circumstances and situations.

Therefore, when we go through the episodic moments of life that's not pleasurable, God is being involved in our situations. Isn't it good to know that God has the solution to your struggles, setbacks, strains, suffering, and etc.? God is governing and involved in your situations.

David writes to the Lord, the one who gives him everything he needs for his journey called life. In like manner, He does the same things for us, He satisfies our needs, heals our bodies, provides for our necessities, protects us from our enemies, rebukes us, restores us, and revives us. He's a healer, a provider, a protector, a banner, a restorer, and a reconciler (this list goes on and on) God is to be. God gives us what we need and then some. He also gives us what we desire. In Him abides the abundant life and absolute truth. When we encounter calamitous situations, He always has the answer to any problem we experience. Do you know the Lord? If not, you need to know Him. With regards to this psalm, if you're going to know Him, then you must have a relationship with Him based on His terms and conditions and not your own. You must be saved (born again). If the believer is going to have an authentic relationship with God, then they must accept Him as Lord and Savior of their lives.

Knowing God is key. Some conclude that they know God, but how can you know God if you have no relationship with Him? If anyone can make such a testimony like David, then they must have a relationship with God. How can you say who He is and what He does if you don't know Him? Additionally, theology teaches that God can be known and He's also incomprehensible.

Some people have no relationship with God whatsoever and claim they have a genuine relationship with God just by knowing Him. Scripture does not support such a statement. Jesus says in John's gospel John 10:27 (NKJV): "My sheep hear My voice, and I know them, and they follow Me." Jesus declares that His sheep hear His voice *phōné*; this means that His sheep obey His voice because they know the Shepherd because of their relationship. Back to the sheep farm, as the shepherdess was talking with me, she began to tour me around the farm, and as we stopped in front of sheep, something powerful happened. She said, "Pastor Young, call them by these names." And I called the sheep by their names and they paid me no attention!

However, when she began to call them, she said, "Watch this, Pastor Young." As she called them, the sheep got up quickly and ran toward her.

She asked, "Pastor Young, do you notice the sheep did not pay you any attention?"

I said, "Yes, ma'am, because I'm not their shepherd and my voice is totally foreign to them."

She said, "Yes, you are right, because the sheep know their shepherd's voice, and this is what Jesus meant."

In addition, the blessing is not only do they know the voice of their shepherd, they, too, follow the voice of their shepherd. It's good to know your shepherd.

The theological term referred to is known as the "knowability of God." Jesus stated once again in John's gospel John 14:7 (NKJV): "If you had known Me, you would have known My Father also; and from now on, you know Him and have seen Him."

Jesus states, "If you had known Me," which means that He can be known or He cannot be known.

If a person is going to have a purposeful, powerful, practical, and personal relationship with God, they will understand what David was saying about a shepherd/sheep connection. He confirms what the Shepherd does for the sheep. In fact, David has the experience of a shepherd himself. He actually understands what a shepherd does for the sheep because he was a shepherd to his father's sheep. When Samuel was searching for a king in Bethlehem at Jesse's house, he examined all of David's brothers, but he knew instinctively they were not the one. He asks Jesse was there another son remaining, and Jesse stated there was only one remaining.

It is recorded in 1 Samuel 16:11 (NKJV):

> And Samuel said to Jesse, "Are all the young men here?" Then he said, "There remains yet the youngest, and there he is, keeping the sheep." And Samuel said to Jesse, "Send and bring him. For we will not sit down till he comes here."

Jesse responded to Samuel and said that he was keeping the sheep, which means that David served in some form of shepherding sheep. Did you catch that? He's shepherding sheep. David was functioning in a camouflage capacity before he was confirmed to calling. God has a meticulous way of concealing you before revealing you. From a spiritual perspective, David sees God as his shepherd and links God to what he did with his sheep in the natural; God in like manner does for him in the spiritual.

Do you know the Lord wants to have a relationship with you? In fact, He wants to have a personal relationship, a provisional relationship, a productive relationship, and a protective relationship, and all of that concerns you. Now since you have a relationship with the Lord, you have something special. When you have the Lord as your Shepherd, He wants to be Lord of all, because if He's not Lord of all, He cannot be your Lord at all.

David has courage and confidence in the Lord. In fact, David has so much confidence that he knows what the Lord is to him and what He does for him. David testifies personally that the Lord is his shepherd. This testimony means that David knows the Lord is his leader, and he, in fact, is the follower. The question is why is the Lord his shepherd? Because David is sheep. David begins this masterpiece of scripture by understanding he and his Shepherd have a relationship together.

When we think about the Shepherd, what should we gather that is so profound about the shepherd/sheep connection? The profound connection is understanding the identity of God in His shepherding character. David says, "The Lord is my shepherd," *Jehovah-Rohi*, which means "shepherd," which further implies He's a companion, He tends, and He protects. A shepherd has a firm connection with the sheep. God is our Shepherd, our feeder, leader, sustainer, and since He does these things as our Shepherd, we must know that we have a Shepherd in God and He tenderly takes care of His sheep.

While in a relationship, do you know what you have in the relationship on the other's behalf? Like having a healthy marriage, relationship has multiple benefits. Having a healthy work relationship has many benefits as well; in fact, also, social relationships have many benefits. In like manner, so does our spiritual relationship have multiple benefits. In our spiritual relationship, we have a relationship with the Lord God Almighty. This relationship will be healthy or unhealthy because it is predicated how well the sheep follow the Shepherd and listen to His voice. The question I'd like to ask is, Do you have a healthy relationship with The Lord? If so, you have benefits when you have the Lord our Shepherd and have the right relationship with Him.

Those who have the right relationship with the Lord will be abundantly blessed. The Lord gives those who are sheep special blessings that those who are not sheep do not obtain because they have an unhealthy or no relationship with Him. Therefore, when you have a relationship with the Lord, your relationship with Him abodes in abundance. Furthermore, know that having a healthy relationship with God has many blessings because the Lord gives special benefits to those who have a healthy relationship with Him.

When you experience lack, the Shepherd is willing to give and meet the needs of His sheep. Whatever we lack, God is eager and ready to lend the necessities to the lacking reservoirs of our lives. We must remember: when we are poor, He's rich; when we are weak, He's strong; when we do not know, He knows. The Lord is abundant in all His provisional blessings which He gives to His children. For we must know He knows how to bless us, He knows how to keep us, He knows how to sustain us, He knows how to provide for us, and He knows how to protect us. If we know that He is our Shepherd, then we must believe whatever we need, He can supply and give us even more.

God always blesses us. Sometimes we may not be aware of it or acknowledge it, but He always gives sufficient supply for His sheep. We are appointed by God and belong to Him. Therefore, He, the Lord, will continually, consistently, and courteously bless and keep us and supply sufficiently according to our needs.

The blessing God gives us is His providence. Sheep should know although they may be unaware they have their Shepherd's providence. As the Shepherd protects the sheep, although the sheep may not be aware of it, their Shepherd is giving them His providence. God gives us His providence governing the affairs of our lives.

Observing the doctrine of providence is very interesting, and it explains in very vital ways how God our Shepherd tends His sheep. Wayne Grudem says God's Providence is: "The doctrine of God's providence has a continuation of His involvement in all things. He involves His continuation in all things by allowing them to exist and be sustained, He continues His cooperation with them while causing them to act a certain way, He continues them by directing them and allowing them to fulfill and complete their purpose."

The Shepherd which the sheep testifies about is the Lord. He gives the sheep His providence and sustains, maintains, and directs them in fulfilling their purpose under His care. God, in fact, sustains His sheep, maintains His sheep, and also directs His sheep. Therefore, we must know that God does something for the sheep that they cannot do for themselves. The Lord is our Shepherd because He gives us His providence and gives us the essentials we need in order to survive. Let's look at some Biblical evidence in God's Word and recognize His providence.

Scripture teaches in Hebrews 1:3 that Christ upholds all things by the word of His power. The Hebrew author's intent is for those who believe, is that Christ upholds all things, which implies He carries all things on His Word. The Greek word *phero* means "to carry or bear." God carries or bears all things by His Word. Another facet of God's providence is recorded in Colossians 1:17 which states, "He is above all things, and in Him, all things consist. Christ is above all things which means that Christ is before all things in the universe."

The prior verse indicates that Christ is the creator of all things that are created in heaven and the earth, visible and invisible, whether thrones or dominions or principalities or powers. All things were created through Him and for Him. Christ the Good Shepherd upholds all things and He is upholding all things by the power of His word. In addition, another perspective of God's providence is documented in Acts 17:28, "For in Him we live and move and have our being." Without God, Luke writes, we cannot even move because He gives us life and mobility. The Greek word *zao* is translated "live," which means "to live," and is derived from the word *biography* which means, "We cannot make it without God because He is the reason we are living and because of such grace our biography is written." Also, the Greek word *kineo* is translated "move" which means "to stir and to put in motion." This indicates that God not only is for our living, also He's responsible for our movements in life as well. Therefore, we cannot even move if it were not approved by God's providence.

The doctrine of God's Providence teaches in this regard, God preserves. Actually, the *Providence of God* means, "God preserves His children and gives the essentials and provides the resources for their earthly assignments." Some individuals have the audacity to assume they accumulated all the additional things in life on their own. This type of thinking is definitely insolent because we are the recipients of God's Providence. Therefore no one should think arrogantly because, without God, we don't exist.

This psalm is a blessing to the sheepfold because it displays the attributes of God from different perspectives that ultimately benefit us. This lyrical masterpiece gives evidence of how God gives His sheep a multiplicity of blessings. In fact, there's a series of divine blessings that have been experienced by the sheep that's given by the Shepherd to meet the sheep's needs in totality. Let's see how the providence of God (Shepherd) works in the lives of the sheep and recognize what He does for them as well, thus, giving the sheep a personal testimony.

Part One

He Guides Us

A Psalm of David. The LORD is my shepherd; I shall not want.

He makes me to lie down in green pastures; He leads me beside the still waters. He restores my soul; He leads me in the paths of righteousness For His name's sake.

—Psalm 23:1-3

The sheep personally testifies that the Shepherd meets our essential needs. There's no one who meets needs like God. He meets our needs with excellence and proficiency. The provisional need the Shepherd supplies is what I call the essential needs. He takes care of our essential needs by guiding us to a place of essentiality. The question must be asked, how does the Shepherd guide the sheep? Since the Shepherd is God, He guides them with the best guidance ever, with no flaws, no faults, or failures, because He's God. No one, absolutely no one, can guide like God can.

There is no comparison to the guidance of God. God provides us with the best care for guidance. David understands very well because of his shepherding experience of his father's sheep. David shares in the shepherding experience; he understands that the Shepherd guides His sheep with excellence and integrity. With that being said, sheep, in fact, need a Shepherd. The Shepherd is vital to the supply of the sheep, and no sheep can follow a Shepherd unless it allows the Shepherd to guide them. Why do sheep need guidance? They are considered to be dumb; therefore, they need to be directed and led by the Shepherd because they are labeled unintelligent. Although sheep are diagnosed as unintelligent and they are in need of a shepherd, just as this is true in nature, it's also true spiritually. In this psalm, David declares the importance of the relational bond between the Shepherd and sheep. David says, "The LORD is my shepherd; I shall not want" (Ps. 23:1, NKJV). David confirms in his relationship with the Shepherd, that he is sheep and God is the Shepherd. He actually confesses that the Lord is "his" Shepherd. The Hebrew word for shepherd, *rā'āh*, means "to tend, to care for, to feed, and to protect." David acknowledges that God is his Shepherd because He tends to his needs, cares for him, feeds him, and gives him shepherding protection. Therefore, God, his feeder, does things for him that he could not do for himself. So, then, when you and I have an authentic relationship with the Shepherd, He gives us the "extras" in our package, because a shepherd always has the best interest for their sheep.

God knows how to make a decision and allow His purpose to work for you because He's God and He doesn't need any help at being Himself. Therefore, we must never get tired of God's blessings because He always supplies awesomely for His sheep. He guides us because, by nature, sheep need to be led and put in the right pasture for nourishment. Therefore, God leads and guides His sheep with the necessary things that are needed for them to be led. All of us need guidance. Yes, all of us do, and all that we need God specializes, tailors, and designs in His unique character to guide us. Have you ever been led to a place of discomfort and disease? In this psalm, David is suggesting that God will guide us into the right places of our lives and give the essentials for our journey.

God knows that we have a desire to be led, but the danger is we can be led in all types of directions. However, we should allow God to lead us and yield to His leading. God is a God of excellence and He knows exactly what He's doing as He leads, guides, and directs us to fulfill our destiny. There are many persons who never fulfill their destiny because they have no guidance. When you have a leader or director, they direct or lead because they perhaps see the potential you possess within, and they want to unleash that very thing that gives you purpose.

Why then is it important that sheep have a shepherd? As I studied the nature of sheep, one of the fascinating things I learned about sheep was "their vision." While studying sheep, I discovered the importance of why sheep in nature have to have a shepherd—it's due to their visual perception. Innately, sheep depend on their vision strongly. It is in the sovereign design of the Creator. He created sheep eyes a certain way. The eyeball of sheep is placed on the side of their head due to giving them the advantage to see predators when they approach them. As a matter of fact, with minimal head movement, they are able to scan their surroundings to see if there are predators in their vicinity. Indeed, with having perception benefits from the Creator, sheep have wide-ranging vision.

On the other hand, I discovered through further research another fascinating thing about the vision of sheep. And then it hit me from a spiritual perspective, why sheep need a shepherd. Sheep actually have poor depth perception. Let alone, their vision is seemingly worse when their heads are up and especially when moving. In addition, they have visionary difficulty when it comes to determining small objects. Actually, when moving, they have to stop and survey their surroundings to see clearly. Granted, they have this problem because of their three-dimensional vision, and when they are mobile, they have extreme trouble viewing their habitat with accuracy. The three-dimensional vision also gives sheep visionary difficulty in regards to viewing shadows (they normally stay away from shadows), they also are unwilling to enter a place they cannot see.

Interestingly enough some have concluded that sheep are color blind. Are sheep color blind? Do they see the same as humans? With the positives and negatives of sheep visionary issues; research shows that sheep, in fact, do see color. However, it's different from the perception of humans. Let me explain the best I can. It is said through studies and test, that sheep see with 20:60 vision and humans see with 20:20 vision, the difference is, sheep color content and human beings color content is surely on the contrary. Factually, with the different color content between sheep and humans, there appears to be something the shepherd sees that the sheep apparently does not see. Through the eyes of sheep, humans look blurry and as far as grass is concerned, green grass in the eyes of sheep has a yellow or brown content. For this reason, sheep see another way but experience a different way (will discuss later).

Another area I've studied in the nature of sheep is their hearing capacity. Interestingly enough, research shows, sheep actually have exceptional hearing. They have the propensity to hear exactly where sounds come from. Sheep can also somehow amplify sound with their hearing and this causes loud noises which scare and spook them. As a result, when sheep hear loud noises, it seems unnatural to them, and when they hear it, they become intensely nervous and very difficult to control. Therefore, when this occurs, the shepherd would talk to the sheep very quietly and calm them down. In addition, sheep have a restrictive response to loud noise because of their stress hormones, and when the shepherd calmly talks to it, its hormones are released and the sheep returns to its calm state. Although we do not know how sheep distinguish between human voices versus animal voices;

however, from the evidence of data, it shows that sheep have good hearing and from a scriptural perspective, they definitely hear their shepherd. Therefore, they need the shepherd's provision.

Divine Provision

The shepherd David speaks about is a provisional Shepherd, He provides. David gives a strong personal testimony about the provisional care of his Shepherd. In fact, he's so connected with the Shepherd, he knows that being in want is not an issue because he never experiences lack. God is not a God of lack. He's more than enough to meet our needs. David even goes to the extent of declaring his Shepherd provides him with every essential thing that's appropriate for him. As a matter of fact, David says his Shepherd leads him. Subsequently, if we are going to model David's attitude toward his Shepherd, then we must allow Him to lead us as well. With this intention, if we make the imperative decision of allowing Him to lead, He then gives a series of divine blessings, and the first thing the Shepherd does for the sheep is give them divine provision.

David testifies he's not in lack by wanting anything because his Shepherd supplies for personal needs. He admits he's not in want which is the Hebrew word *hāsēr* which means to be in lack or decrease or without. He firmly acknowledges he doesn't have to worry because his wants are not in things, but his desire is in God. Do you recall that David was a man after God's own heart? Besides, he's focused upon his God and since he's connected to the Shepherd, the Shepherd has everything he needs because God has enough to not only meet his needs, but to also exceed his expectations!

God exceeds David's expectations due to the fact that he's not in any lack whatsoever. This is indeed because of the provision God gives to His sheep. David actually testifies, "I'm not in lack at all or of any kind because the Lord fills the lack with provision." In other words, David expresses he's cared for totally and he actually never realizes what lack is because God gives him provision. David glorifies God to the fullest because he never viewed God as the resource, he looked to God as the *source*!

In fact, He gives the resource, and the resource comes from Him because He's the source! A resource is never more valuable than the Source. God is the one who supplies the needs of His people simply because He's a God of provision. Above all, when He provides for the sheep, it demonstrates His care and His compassionate characteristics. He cares for us with such compassion and favor. Indeed, no one can compare to the provisionary craftsmanship of the Shepherd when it comes to providing for the sheep. Therefore, when sheep need the provision of the Shepherd, they somehow understand that the Shepherd is relevant to their circumstance, and they need the shepherd for their leadership and survival. To add, they also recognize that the shepherd gives them the necessities of nurture, nourishment, and never neglect. God's shepherding power reveals His provision and exposes the reality of Him being the life-giver king.

From a spiritual perspective, we who are sheep know that God is the supplier of life. He gives us constant provisions and supplies our needs. The Shepherd (God) provides the sheep with what they need and also desire. The Shepherd will always bless the sheep with provisionary blessings; therefore, they have no worries because they understand their Shepherd will supply all their necessities.

David shares an honest statement when he declares that he shall not want. Not being in want simply means he's not in lack of anything. Why? Because the Lord is his Shepherd. One who experiences no lack knows they have something special and that specialness comes from God. We have provision. The word *hāsēr* or "not want" which is a verb indicating to be lacking, to be needy; to decrease. David says that he will not be in lack, needy, or decrease because the Lord is his Shepherd.

We cannot say that God doesn't care for His children because He cares for us all. Therefore, if we know He cares for us, then we should cast all our cares on Him because the Lord supplies for His creation. In addition, we have in God a Shepherd, leader, provider, and so much more. In order to know what God does for His sheep, one must have a revelation of who God is in their life. Whereas, we must have the instinct to know that the Shepherd has the power, authority, and capability to lead His sheep into the places where they would prosper and be protected.

Now, let's be honest we want God to take care of us. There is something within us that causes us to want, we call it, desire. All of us have desire, aspirations and a drive, you can't deny that. There's something within us that demands great desire, and it compels us to have a hunger to receive what has been absent in our lives. Believe it or not, someone is always wanting something, whether it's success, prosperity, accomplishments, good health, and etc., we are agents of wanting. When you purchased your home, vehicle, and the extras, you bought them because there was a wanting or desire within.

We have a heart's desire to do something that's adventurous, to attain something we feel incomplete in or unfulfilled. In fact, there's an inner push or drive that capitalizes a craving within. Subsequently, we discover through the different experiences and encounters, that God is the answer to our aspirations. The reason why our lack is covered is that God always gives perfect and precise provision in any season.

In difficult seasons, we must trust in the Shepherd's ability to take us to the next level of our lives. With that being said, God provides for His sheep and gives them an abundance of blessings that puts them under the awareness of knowing they are in the right place and under the right care. God actually provides for us daily and when we face life's moments that seem like He's abandoned us, we must remember the words of Christ, that is, "He will never leave us nor forsake us." Furthermore, we should be overjoyed because God's presence is persistent and practical in our lives.

In this current culture, we can understand His provisional care as providing in the midst of a recession. We experienced a recession and God showed us that He can supply for the sheep and that no earthly setback can hinder His supply for His sheep because God is not subject to the laws of this world because the earth is the Lord's and the fullness thereof. He's God; no one can control Him, contain Him, constrain Him, nor corrupt Him. He takes care of us. Just as an earthly shepherd cares for his sheep, so does God, being our spiritual Shepherd takes care of us as well.

The custom of shepherds in the east was to care for their flock, find pasture for them, water for them when they were thirsty, and they would also protect them from their predators. In relation to God, He has a consistent supply for His sheep and He provides faithfully for them as He supplies their every need. What do you think about divine provision? Do you trust totally in the Shepherd's care for His sheep? Do you believe your Shepherd knows what He's doing? It doesn't matter what your situation is, God knows what's best for you. When experiencing provision, one must realize that the provider is the giver of resources that has been allotted to such.

We can certainly attest that God has an overflow of tremendous provision. His divine provision plays a vital role in our lives. God has provided in so many ways for us, just as the earthly shepherd provides for the sheep. He renders a supply that cannot be duplicated, matched, or rivaled. In 2008, we went through an economic famine when gas prices were soaring through the roof (and still are), high foreclosures rates, loss of jobs, and etc. He provided. Often when it comes to the provisionary ways of God, sometimes we may not realize that God has our backs and meets our needs. Although there are times when we think that God will not provide, but He shows us that He can provide for us and render Shepherding care to make us complete.

It's absolutely amazing that you and I have the provision of God in our lives. Do you believe that you are a recipient of God's provision? I must tell you, there's good news, you are a recipient of the provision of God. That's why you should never give up to the pressures and perplexities of life because God is a persistent provider. He provides the necessities for the sheep. In addition, He also provides our essentials. Have you ever been in a place where you assumed that your necessities and essentials would not meet? But you continued your trust in the leadership of your Shepherd and He put you not in a place of ridicule but of peace. This is what divine provision is all about, God puts His children in their rightful place for a rightful purpose for His rightful plan.

When you are under His divine provision, God strategically puts you in the right place. Where is the place of provision? It's called nothing lacking. When you are connected to the Shepherd then you will have the benefits of the Shepherd to experience the blessings which I call divine provision.

The psalmist expresses praises unto God because he had experienced His provision. You and I have as well experienced the provisionary ways of God, and we should honor Him with praise because He has provided for us in so many ways. God has provided with excellent care, anointed care, appointed care. What does divine provision do for the sheep? It gives them care that they may even not be aware of. Sheep by nature cannot take themselves to a place of provision; they need a shepherd to do that. They need a shepherd to lead them to a place of provision, peace, and prosperity. Sheep need to be led to the place where their shepherd can put them in a place of necessity and nourishment.

God provides us with what we need for the provisionary experience. When He leads you into the provisionary experience, understand that's what He does—lead. This is why it's so important to understand the Lord will not lead you to a place where there is no prosperity, provision, peace, and protection. When you encounter His provision, you have in reality what

He has permitted sovereignly. That's why when you have the connected blessing, you have what humanity cannot give but divinity supplies. The things you thought you were not worthy of being blessed with, God gave you and led you to that place of provision; the job you were not qualified for, but God led you to the provision to get the job; when you received healing from that terminal disease, God led you to the place of healing. When you have been led, you will be fed. God's provision makes an imperative difference in our lives because sheep do not contain the capacity to lead themselves; therefore, they need the leadership of the shepherd. Spiritually speaking, sheep need to follow the Shepherd in order to be led to their spiritual purpose and provisions He has ordained for their spiritual pilgrimage. In fact, sheep really have no productive purpose if they do not follow the shepherd. David mentions the Lord leads him. This is how we are led into provision because we simply follow His leadership.

What will sheep experience when they encounter The Shepherd's care? They will experience the no-lack life by being led to the luxury of green pastures. The psalmist says that the sheep are led to green pastures by being made to lie down in green pastures to experience the goodness of the shepherd. Oriental shepherds did not drive their sheep, they led them. As being led to provision, the shepherd would lead the sheepfold to green pastures to lie down. It is in green pastures. The shepherd's desire for his sheep is to be in a place of peace. David testifies that the Lord, "makes him to lie in green pastures and leads him besides the still waters."

The word David uses for lead is *nāhal*, which denotes to guide along. Also, it has the sense of guiding people, leading them in an orderly fashion and with great care. That's what a shepherd is—a guide, feeder, and protector with the sole purpose of providing great care for the flock, while He executes His job description. The Lord leads us in an orderly fashion. He leads us into the places of our lives that causes us to encounter His purpose for our lives through His providence. As scripture says in Psalm 37:23 (NKJV), "The steps of a good man are ordered by the Lord, And He delights in his way." The Shepherd orders the sheep steps due to His awareness of leadership. As the Lord orders the steps of a man, what actually takes place? According to this particular text, the word 'order' kûn means to set up, to make firm, to establish, to prepare and to set in place.

This is what essential leadership does when one is being led into their provisionary purpose. The Shepherd has the best intentions for the sheep and He leads them to the best pasture He has predestined for them. He has a place of rest and relaxation for His sheep and their position of rest is evident that they enjoy the Shepherd's provision. The Shepherd's order and vision are extremely important because without it we cannot be set in the territory of provision.

While in the territory of provision the sheep are experiencing the Shepherd's awesome favor. While experiencing His favor, it doesn't mean there will never be problems, setbacks, and conflict because there certainly will be. Therefore, when going through these episodic situations, there is no need to worry or be afraid because the Lord will have you in a place of rest and relaxation because it's not accidental, it's intentional. When you are led into a place of rest and relaxation, you will be fed there as well. Eastern shepherds led sheep into green pastures because they could receive the best grass for grazing. The Shepherd provides the absolute best for His sheep and they enjoy it!

However, the complex contrast is, as I stated earlier, sheep see green grass as yellow or brown. With that being said, sheep are in a place better than what they see. Once again, they see green as yellow or brown. Therefore, this is indicative of their sight; their seeing experience is different from their actual experience. "What do you mean?" I guess you are saying. Well, you see, they see yellow or brown grass, but it's green according to the human eye. Now, since they (sheep) are in a pasture of yellow grass in their eyes but actually green in human eyes, there's a difference in the grass and it's the texture.

There's certainly a difference in the texture of yellow or brown grass than green. The difference in the texture of the grasses is concluding what's nourishing and what's not. For we know that yellow or brown grass has no texture, it's flaky, damaged, and appears to be dead. Although in all actuality, yellow or brown grass is not dead, it just has no nutrients, also it can be dormant. There's a difference in the texture. On the other hand, green grass has texture, life, nutrition, and substance. It's evident why shepherds did not lead sheep to yellow or brown pastures because of the absence of nourishment. The reality is yellow or brown pastures have lacking nutrients, deficiencies due to an overpopulation of insects, and possibly difficult locations for growing grass. It also could choke the sheep if they chewed it.

However, green grass has the right nutrients, proteins, no lacking deficiencies, control of insect population and the grass grows. Shepherds lead sheep to green pastures because they supply the essential necessities for them. When sheep experience the green pastures, they experience the "sheep" good life. Historically, green pastures were an oasis of rich and grassier fields. However, the contrasting element about green grass and yellow or brown grass is that green grass is tender, pleasant, and a great source of food for sheep. As I stated earlier, sheep have a seeing experience and an actual experience.

While they see yellow or brown grass (which, from a human perspective, is dormant or dead), they are actually eating green, textured, nourished, tender, and pleasant grass. That goes without saying, spiritually speaking, God always does something for us that we see one way but experience in another. His provisions that we experience are from divinity and distributed to humanity. Therefore, we cannot comprehend what God the Shepherd does because our ways are not His and His ways are not ours. The prophet Isaiah says, Isaiah 55:8 (NKJV), "'For My thoughts are not your thoughts, Nor are your ways My ways,' says the LORD."

Sheep do not know actually how their shepherd provides for them, but he does. There are many ways we have seeing experiences and actual experiences. You may not be totally qualified for the job, but the job is yours. You may have thought your credit was not good enough to attain something you needed, but it ended up in your possession. Your confidence was hurt when you received the bad news from the doctor's report, but you are a living testimony. In addition, your faith was tested during a conflicting challenge, however, your confidence in the Shepherd caused you to stay steadfast and unmovable. Those are some of the seeing experiences we encounter although what keeps us in awe about God is, we at times see one experience but encounter another.

When nurture, nourishment, and necessity have met, it puts the sheepfold in a place of treasurable tranquility. This is why when they experience the provision of the Shepherd, they see the vision of the Shepherd leads them to a higher level or dimension of His shepherding care, and that is experiencing provision peacefully.

When we focus on divine provision, there is a scriptural account of the provision of God we should notice. The account in Genesis about Abraham and Isaac is the epitome of what divine provision is about. In this account, the name of God is experienced under the umbrella of His provision.

> Now it came to pass after these things that God tested Abraham, and said to him, "Abraham!" And he said, "Here I am."
>
> Then He said, "Take now your son, your only son, Isaac, whom you love, and go to the land of

Moriah, and offer him there as a burnt offering on one of the mountains of which I shall tell you."

So Abraham rose early in the morning and saddled his donkey, and took two of his young men with him, and Isaac his son; and he split the wood for the burnt offering, and arose and went to the place of which God had told him.

Then on the third day Abraham lifted his eyes and saw the place afar off.

And Abraham said to his young men, "Stay here with the donkey; the lad and I will go yonder and worship, and we will come back to you."

So Abraham took the wood of the burnt offering and laid it on Isaac his son; and he took the fire in his hand, and a knife, and the two of them went together.

But Isaac spoke to Abraham his father and said, "My father!" And he said, "Here I am, my son." Then he said, "Look, the fire and the wood, but where is the lamb for a burnt offering?"

And Abraham said, "My son, God will provide for Himself the lamb for a burnt offering." So the two of them went together.

Then they came to the place of which God had told him. And Abraham built an altar there and placed the wood in order; and he bound Isaac his son and laid him on the altar, upon the wood.

And Abraham stretched out his hand and took the knife to slay his son.

But the Angel of the LORD called to him from heaven and said, "Abraham, Abraham!" So he said, "Here I am."

And He said, "Do not lay your hand on the lad, or do anything to him; for now I know that you fear God, since you have not withheld your son, your only son, from Me."

Then Abraham lifted his eyes and looked, and there behind him was a ram caught in a thicket by its horns. So Abraham went and took the ram, and offered it up for a burnt offering instead of his son.

And Abraham called the name of the place, The-LORD-Will-Provide; as it is said to this day, "In the Mount of The LORD it shall be provided." (Gen. 22:1–14, NKJV)

Abraham has been tested by God to perform a specific sacrifice of his own flesh and blood. One may ask the question, Why would God tell Abraham to actually kill his biological son? To add, Abraham was asked by Isaac, "Where is the lamb for the burnt offering?" Abraham responds and promises Isaac that God will provide. Abraham has faith in the provision of God in a perplexing moment. While he gets ready to slay his son, an angel speaks out and tells Abraham to stop because a substitute sacrifice is stuck in the thicket.

Abraham gets the ram that is stuck in the thicket and sacrifices it, and then he utters the provisionary name of God. Abraham calls Him *yehōwāh yir'eh* which means literally "The Lord will see to it," it also means "The God who provides." It's actually good to know that we worship a God who's dependable, trustworthy, and reliable and He sees to it. He is a see-to-it God. He will see to it that He will provide what is needed for His children. God has many ways of providing. Just as He provided for Abraham, He will provide for us as well. So then, never underestimate what God can do because when it seems impossible, He makes it possible because He specializes in all things.

The psalmist describes the Shepherd as a provider. Therefore, if we desire the provision of God, please know that He's able to provide it, divine provision. We should never doubt what God can do for His sheep because when we feel like we've lost, we've actually won. My friend, you've won because you have a relationship with God. Sheep have a Shepherd for a reason, the Shepherd leads them to a place of provision. Therefore, we should be encouraged because David suggests that his Shepherd is a giver and He will provide what's needed when needed.

There's another example of divine provision recorded in scripture. It is the Biblical account with the children of Israel, it says in Deuteronomy 2:7 (KJV):

> For the LORD thy God hath blessed thee in all the works of thy hand: he knoweth thy walking through this great wilderness: these forty years the LORD thy God hath been with thee; thou hast lacked nothing. As the Israelites traveled they were commanded by God to take certain turns to get to the Promise Land. While on their journey they experienced the provision of God and they

18

lacked nothing. I cannot say this enough, "God gives provision to His children.

He makes ways possible for us to experience His divine provision.

In addition, one of my favorites in all of Scripture shows us the provision of God when He provided for Elijah in a famine.

> And Elijah the Tishbite, who was of the inhabitants of Gilead, said unto Ahab, As the LORD God of Israel liveth, before whom I stand, there shall not be dew nor rain these years, but according to my word.
>
> And the word of the LORD came unto him, saying,
>
> Get thee hence, and turn thee eastward, and hide thyself by the brook Cherith, that is before Jordan.
>
> And it shall be, that thou shalt drink of the brook; and I have commanded the ravens to feed thee there.
>
> So he went and did according unto the word of the LORD: for he went and dwelt by the brook Cherith, that is before Jordan.
>
> And the ravens brought him bread and flesh in the morning, and bread and flesh in the evening; and he drank of the brook.

And it came to pass after a while, that the brook dried up, because there had been no rain in the land.

And the word of the LORD came unto him, saying,

Arise, get thee to Zarephath, which belongeth to Zidon, and dwell there: behold, I have commanded a widow woman there to sustain thee. (1 Kings 17:1–9, KJV)

In this text, Elijah prophesizes and declares that there will be no dew nor rain for these years. According to tradition (James 5:17), the drought lasted three and a half years. However, Elijah becomes a victim of his own prophecy. But while the famine persists, God provides for Elijah. In the process of His provisional encounter, He tells Elijah to "turn eastward and hide by the brook Cherith that's right before Jordan." Although there's a dry season, God provides for Elijah by commanding the ravens to feed him there. Also, he does not have to search for water because he's by the brook. However, over a period of time, the brook dries up because there was no rain in the land. And the Lord speaks to him and tells him, "To go to Zarephath because He has commanded a widow woman to sustain him there."

Now I must confess, this is very encouraging because the narrative shows us that God helps us survive dry seasons. In every phase of our lives, God will give His children divine provision, allowing them to not lack anything. That's what the Shepherd does for the sheep, He provides. We can certainly attest that God has given provision to us on a daily basis. You and I have what we need for this pilgrimage called life because God gives us the victory over lack. In Him we have everything we need.

When you look back over your life, you can see the provision of God. Having the right relationship with Him, possessing relevant resources from Him, and experiencing required rest comes from His umbrella of provision. David understands the power of encountering the provision of God because he has the right relationship with God. God will always meet His children's needs, He will give us relevant resources (things to experience that doesn't show lack) to survive, yes, even in dry seasons. David understands also that God gives Him required rest which implies that God will put him in a habitat that is conducive for rest that the Shepherd requires for the sheep. John Calvin says in his commentary on the psalms concerning this psalm, "Under the similitude of a shepherd, he commends the care which God, in his providence, had exercised toward him." God, my friend, has given provision toward you and me; therefore, in like manner, just as the earthly shepherd cares for his flock, so does God care for His sheep.

Divine Peace

Sheep are very meticulous animals. They are animals that love to dwell in something most human beings seem to have lost, and that's peace. Sheep do not like controversy. They like to dwell in herds while grazing, and they become irritated if the flock is separated. They are also very social; it's against sheep nature to be antisocial if you see a group of sheep grazing together (perhaps in small numbers), they would normally have a relationship.

In addition, in reference to their social behavior, they love to flock together, and this implies they are animals of unity. When there is unity, there is the experience of strength, also there's peace. Sheep love to dwell in a certain vicinity to solidify their peace and tranquility. They love green pastures. While in green pastures, they have the presence of the shepherd and they encounter a season of deserved peace. Isn't it good to go through a seasonal period where you experience deserved peace? When predators are off limits, when insects are not irritating (they are to sheep), when unity is in the flock, when rest is relevant, when satisfaction is normal, when the anointing is present, and when rest is actually relaxing. Now, my friends, it's good to have deserved peace, but it's far better to have the intimate connection to be overshadowed with divine peace.

What is divine peace? It is the God kind of peace God gives to His sheep to experience and encounter rest. The psalmist declares the shepherd makes him lie down in green pastures. Experiencing the green pasture life is evidence of the shepherd's care for the sheep. As mentioned earlier, rest and relaxation is part of the green pasture life. However, there's an addition to the rest and relaxation, and that is peace. The Shepherd gives sheep peace in their green pasture experience. What did sheep experience when they encountered divine peace in a vicinity of rest and relaxation? They had an encounter with peace. The aim of the shepherd was to not only provide a place of provision for the sheep, but one of peace as well.

When sheep experience green pasture moments, they are in a peaceful state. When shepherds led their sheep into green pastures, they actually placed them in a grassier vicinity, which was a meadow, which implies, more. When the shepherds led sheep to grassier fields, they put them in these pastures for not only rest and relaxation but nourishment. In a season of the green pasture experience, sheep would experience security, serenity, and satisfaction. Have you experienced security, serenity, and satisfaction? If so, you are, my friend, encountering a green pasture experience. The natural characteristic of sheep is to be in a place of peace. Now for an animal who's labeled as unintelligent, at least they have the instinct to have peace. An important factor about green pastures is the location. Every location is not a place of peace; some are places of peril. And there is no peace for sheep in a perilous location.

Sheep enjoy the pleasantness of peace. I believe they are in bliss because they have been led to a place where they didn't have the intelligence to go; they have been led by their shepherd.

Actually, they are where they are because of the guidance of the shepherd. Instinctively, sheep know how to eat, but they do not have the intelligence to put themselves in a place of rest and relaxation. Peace is important to possess, and when sheep are in green pastures, this is the reality of their experience. When sheep go through the process to get to the place where the shepherd sanctioned for them, they actually function from what I call a luxury location.

Sheep, in fact, are in a location of luxury when they have their shepherd amongst them. They feel secure, they are satisfied, and they are in serenity.

Spiritually speaking, when you have the Lord in your life, He gives you security, satisfaction, and serenity. There's no greater feeling than knowing that your provider and protector is in your midst. What feeling will you have, a peaceful one? When you know who leads you, who loves, and who longs for you, you feel peace.

Having the peace of God is essential to possessing divine peace. Paul confessed to the church at Philippi about his experience with the peace of God. Philippians 4:6–7 (NKJV), "Be anxious for nothing, but in everything by prayer and supplication, with thanksgiving, let your requests be made known to God; and the peace of God, which surpasses all understanding, will guard your hearts and minds through Christ Jesus." In reality, Paul belonged to the sheepfold and he was an awesome man of God, but he emphasized how important the peace of God is to believers.

Do you know how valuable the peace of God is in your life? In fact, nothing can compare to having the peace of God in your life. What keeps you when you are confused? God's peace. What contains you when you could be frustrated? The peace of God. What has held you together when things could have fallen apart? Divine peace. What do you have when circumstances are difficult but you still have a calmness about you that no one can comprehend? The peace of the Shepherd. When sheep experience green pastures, they experience peace. Better yet, the peace of their Shepherd.

One thing I've noticed about the shepherd is, he takes sheep to the place of their rightful purpose. Yes, there must be a season when the shepherd takes the sheepfold to a place of purposeful rest, splendor, and satisfaction. Now there comes a time when rest is essential for the body, especially from toil, turbulence, tension, and strain. Your body needs to be recharged, rebooted, and rekindled. This is done by taking the proper rest one needs by having the discipline to do so. So then, the shepherd takes time to find the rightful place for the sheep to rest and be renewed.

Now let's not underestimate it; you can be tired physically, mentally, emotionally, and spiritually as well. You can be depleted and need to be restored, revived, and renewed so that you can produce effective results for the kingdom of God. The shepherding care of the shepherd renders compassion to the sheep that they may be rightly restored, and that's only manifested by creating a restful environment. When sheep get in the vicinity of green grass, the shepherd's intent for them is to experience rest. Therefore, while experiencing rest, they will also experience satisfaction, comfort, security, and confidence, all because they are in their rightful place.

Have you never pondered the thought of why rest is so important to those who are extremely busy? I look at this passage as a vacation. When you go on vacation, you save a desired amount of money for the purpose of enjoying your vacation. You find the best place for lodging accommodations. Travel to the desired destination and not worry about what's going on at home and what bill you'd have to pay when you return. No, you're not even worried about the positives and negatives, you just want to get away. And when you get away, you have a season of rest and tranquility. Although it is temporary, you need it very much.

In like manner, sheep are in a place where they are not concerned about the awareness of predators, parasites, nor problems because they are in a place of rest. Rest is essential for the process. Sometimes the best thing you can have is rest. But I've noticed something very interesting about the green pastures, and that is, it's a combination. Remember, David gives a testimony about his Shepherd (the Lord), and what He does for him in their relationship. He says, "I shall not want." What's interesting about not being in lack is, whatever process David is in, he understands that the provision of the Shepherd will always be in his life to sustain him.

So then, what's the combination? He has rest and food. In the green pastures, comfort and consumption are being experienced by the sheep. Therefore, sheep do not have to fret because they have what they need from their provisionary giver. While lying in the textured field, they are not in lack, they are in plenty. They have food for their body because their shepherd has guided them to the resources necessary for their purpose.

Now, one of the realities about sheep that cannot be denied is, they are difficult to be made to lie down. It is a known fact that sheep will not lay when they experience certain things: fear is something that causes sheep to be reluctant to lay in the green, textured grass; another is when there is discord among their flock; when there's a rivalry amongst the flock. However, circumstances change when the shepherd comes among them. Yes, the shepherd makes the difference. In our relationship with others, churches, businesses, and establishments will have no unity when there's fear, discord, and rivalries.

The Shepherd is the difference maker for the flock. When the Shepherd is in their vicinity, fear is evicted, discord evaporates, and rivalries are erased due to the presence of the Shepherd. Honestly, it will be difficult to lay in peace when there is fear, when there is discord, and when rivalries are associated with you often. You will never have peace when you are constantly saturated with fear. In addition, you will not have peace when your sheepfold or flock is in a routine of discord. Furthermore, when there are rivalries in the flock, you cannot rest as well; so, the flock needs the shepherd to make a habitat of peace.

Sheep like unity and their instincts show that they are animals of unity and they love a peaceful habitat. Therefore, for the believers of Christ, we should desire to have peace as well. When sheep lie down, they show that there's unity in the flock and their surroundings have to be right for them to lie in peace. How can we lie in peace when our surroundings are not peaceful? You can't. When you are fearful of those who have predatory spirits because of your nature is to be prey, when unwilling sheep are not willing to make adjustments to demolish discord, when dominant sheep pursue sheep rivalries continuously, it's very hard to lie down. Sheep have a specific way of showing they are in a habitat of peace—it's when they chew their cud. When I visited the sheep farm, the shepherdess informed me, saying, "When you see the sheep lying down and chewing on the cud, they are in a state of tranquility. Sheep have a four-chambered stomach, with this type of stomach they are able to regurgitate a food bolus that can be rechewed and re-swallowed, and when doing this they are in a place of tranquility. Furthermore, sheep by nature show there can be no inner harmony if there's outer chaos."

How can you lie in peace when your bills are stacked to the ceiling? How can you lie in peace when your home is almost foreclosed? How can you function sanely in an environment when your doctor's report was not what you expected or wanted to hear? How can you operate as normal when your funny money has become strange change? How can you act as status quo when your family is torn from the floor up? Be honest, you can't. So then, it will become easier to lie in green pastures when the shepherd comes on the scene. The Shepherd gives stability and security to the surrounding habitat, then the flock can rest authentically.

Sheep also feel peace when they are not only in green pastures but beside still waters. As I stated earlier, sheep are very meticulous animals. Although they are considered to be unintelligent, they are, however, scrupulous. The fact that sheep love the vicinity of green pastures, they also are at ease when they see still waters. What gives sheep a sense of calmness when they are beside the still waters? Now in order to understand still waters, we must understand how sheep conduct themselves around the proximity of still waters. Sheep hate movement around them. There's something sheep thrive on having that makes them feel peace and that's refreshment. As the shepherd leads them to green pastures, he also guides them beside still waters. The flock will not rest or be refreshed when they encounter bombarding conflict. However, the conditions of the atmosphere have to be right for them to rest and be refreshed.

Comprehensively, getting a grasp on still waters is very interesting. As the shepherd leads the flock of sheep beside the still waters, what actually happens? The Hebrew word used here, *menûḥāh*, is a feminine noun meaning "resting place, rest, and quiet." This implies that the word *still* refers to quietness and restfulness. Therefore, when sheep encounter the green pasture experience, which is rest, they also encounter still water, which means restoration.

Another important thing to notice is, the word *mayim* is a masculine noun meaning "water, a basic element." Sheep prefer their environment to be a place of quietness, full of rest and restoration. This is what divine peace gives when you've been in a quiet place having been rested and restored. These two essentials are experienced. In addition, you cannot be effective in any endeavor if you do not have the proper rest, because real rest births your restoration.

Rest and restoration are important to sheep because they become agitated when noticing moving water, even in green pastures. They like green pastures, but they also like still waters. Why? Actually, still waters have a quiet sound. Therefore, while in a place full of texture, substance, and nourishment, something

27

is missing, quietness. Although sheep eat and rest in the green textured fields, they also need water, still waters. Still waters seem to be a metaphorical magnet of peace for sheep. Sheep feel restful and safe when they are beside still waters lying in green pastures. While eating the lush of the fields and drinking quiet waters gives the flock peace. Sheep do not like flowing or moving water; they like still waters because moving waters terrifies them. In the east, shepherds have been known to dam up the water flow for it to become still. They wanted to provide the sheep with everything they needed to be in a haven of peace and restoration. Therefore, our Shepherd moves and maneuvers things in our lives for His glory and our benefit just for us to experience peace.

Some eastern fields are rocky and very uncomfortable. However, the shepherds would still find a meadow that would be beneficial for their flock. How many rocky situations have you had in life? But God our Shepherd took us through the rocky and uncomfortable places of life to get us to a place of comfort, rest, and peace. When the shepherds led sheep to rest and restoration, they were taking them to a place to experience their destiny.

Think with me for a moment; think about how God just as earthly shepherds do for their flock think about, how He cares for us? Earthly shepherds would go the extra mile to see that their flock were protected, comforted, and satisfied. As we think about the goodness of God and how He has protected, comforted, and satisfied us, it should allow you to have peace. Therefore, when you know what gives you peace and comfort and who leads you there, you certainly have a combination worth having.

Sheep may be misunderstood by some, and since we are sheep, we will be misunderstood as well. Sheep have instincts and in their arsenal of instincts, they have strange instinctive thrust that sanctions their comfort. Sheep have unfamiliar tendencies, but they are who they are. They know what they need not by intelligence but by instinct. From studying sheep, an additional thing I've noticed in reference to their instincts is they depend on their shepherd. They have a created instinct to confide in the intelligence of their shepherd to meet their needs because instinctively, they don't know how to lead themselves into those rightful places.

The earthly shepherd knows exactly what the sheep's needs are. God is the same way. He knows what we need and He knows what we desire. He knows when we need to be in green pastures and be beside the still waters. God knows how to supply for every iota of your life. Just as shepherds know what's best for their sheep, so does God knows what's best for us. He knows what His children's needs are. When shepherds take their sheep into the vicinity of green pastures and still waters, it's for the purpose for resting the sheep and restoring them.

God desires His sheep to be in a place of pleasure and peace. Honestly, sometimes, life has situations that sometimes don't seem so pleasant and He wants them to be in a restful place. Are you in a restful place? Do you have the ambition to have peace in your life? If so, God will give you peace. You can't go far without rest and restoration. You will burn out. You need it. There are times when we need to slow down, be more observant, and be patient. Sometimes we allow this fast-paced society to influence us and we begin to model our behavior based upon culture. We should be appreciative that God has a Shepherd's heart. The heart of God's compassion and concern for His sheep is encouraging. In fact, when conflicting moments come, it's difficult to rest. Just as sheep, we need things to be peaceful in order to have peace.

David thanks God for the peace that He gives to His children. Actually, his connection with Him has allowed David to know the Shepherd in another relational capacity. No doubt David knows Him as Jehovah-Shalom which denotes, "The LORD is my/our peace; the peace of the LORD." God is the only one who can give true peace. When the Shepherd displays a habitat of peace, the sheep are at peace. A great reference to Jehovah-Shalom is recorded in Judges 6:24 where Gideon built an altar there unto the Lord and called it Jehovah-Shalom.

The shepherd longs for the peace of the flock. The shepherd also desires his sheep to dwell in a peaceful environment. In the east, shepherds would go the extra mile for their flock to be in a peaceful habitat. Shepherds take total care of their sheep and while they lead them to green pastures and still waters, they guide them to a place of restoration. It's very important to be restored and true restoration begins when Jesus Christ has become your Lord and Savior. God wants you to be in a place of total dependence upon Him and when you give Him "yourself," He will lead you into His peace.

Divine Power

On the path of righteousness, the Shepherd gives His sheep complete restoration. We worship a God who restores, revives, and renews His sheep completely. The Hebrew word the psalmist uses, šûḇ, is interesting. It's a verb meaning "to turn, to return, to go back, to do again, to change, to withdraw, to bring back, to reestablish, to be returned, to bring back, to take, to restore, to recompense, to answer." What the Shepherd does for us when we are restored is tremendously awesome. The Shepherd gives us power and this power is not human, it's divine.

When He demonstrates His power unto us, He demonstrates His care. God wants us to return unto Him as we should. His desire for us is change. He wants us to withdraw from negativity and illegitimacy. He wants to reestablish you, restore you, and bring you back to His original design for your life. The emphasis on the word is idiomatic, which means "He puts something new." That's what restoration is all about; it revitalizes you and restores you to your rightful place and purpose holistically!

The Shepherd wants to makes you renewed by putting within you, newness. Just as sheep get agitated in their habitat, so do we find ourselves in places that cause discomfort and discouragement in our environments. Therefore, what must we do when we are at our wits' end and feel exhausted? We must trust in the Shepherd's care and allow Him to lead us and restore us.

David candidly confesses that his soul has been restored, which means healing has begun. He intimately experiences God in a different way of shepherding, and provision he now encounters healing. David knows God in another way. He experiences *Jehovah–Rapha* "The Lord who heals." David understands that when one has an authentic relationship with the Shepherd, they will not only be led and provided for, but when healing and restoration are needed, God will supply it as well.

There are so many people who have a relationship with God, but they have not allowed Him to restore and heal them. One thing the Psalmist states for certain is, healing is not only for the body, it's also for the soul. In fact, *Jehovah–Rapha* heals spiritually, physically, mentally, and emotionally. He gives total restoration. The psalmist wrote the following about healing, Psalm 103:3–5 (NKJV), "Who forgives all your iniquities, Who heals all your diseases, Who redeems your life from destruction, Who crowns you with lovingkindness and tender mercies, Who satisfies your mouth with good things, So that your youth is renewed like the eagle's."

God is a healer. He heals the sick, lame, and blind; He cast out demons and He heals people from their sin. The psalmist also stated another powerful declaration about *Jehovah–Rapha* in Psalm 147:3 (NKJV), "He heals the brokenhearted and binds up their wounds."

Broken-hearted means those whose hearts are shattered. He heals and also wraps their wounds. When you have a Shepherd/sheep connection, you have the benefits of the Shepherd. Healing is, in fact, a benefit that comes from God. Therefore, when one has been restored, they have experienced the healing power of God, they have an encounter with *Jehovah-Rapha*.

31

Never underestimate the power of God. God is powerful and we need His power. We can make it in the dumpster days of life because of God's power. Life has many challenges and some are not easy to endure; therefore, if we rely on the power of God, He will take us through. We need the power of God to propel us to our place of destiny to experience restoration.

There are many people who need to be restored. You've tried things your way for a long time, and as of yet, you have not come to any resolve. You have done things your way and tried to revive yourself within your own power. However, nothing has changed because your power is limited, but if you would turn to the Shepherd, He will give restorative power that will allow you to be whole. Also, there are sheep who have a connection with the Shepherd, and perhaps, over a period of time, have gone contrary to His leadership. What must they do? Repent and allow Him to restore you.

My friends, when you are restored, you are made anew and God gives you restoration and rejuvenates you for a purpose. God has a purpose for His sheep. If they are going to be restored and healed, they must depend on His power and His power alone. You can't depend on the authority of humanity, no, you need divine assistance. The authority of humanity is limited and the authority of divinity is unlimited. Sheep will find themselves lost if they trusted in their own intellect. They need the shepherd.

Jesus Christ our Lord is a healer. There are many scriptural accounts of His healing power. Also, there are accounts not recorded in scripture because He still heals! One of my favorite stories in scripture is about the woman who had the issue of blood for a decade plus two years. This narrative is indeed a blessing because it proves to us about the healing power of God when faith is applied.

This woman has had a horrific experience for twelve years and was in no way getting better. Her condition has actually grown worse Mark 5:25–29. She has had a plethora of problems.

She's bleeding, banned, and broke because she spent all she had and gave it to physicians. She amazingly hears about the power of Jesus Christ, and she becomes encouraged and has a confidential conversation with herself to touch the hem of His garment.

She says within herself according to Matthew's account and has a conversation with herself that if she can touch His hem, she would indeed be made complete. Meanwhile, Jesus is on His way to awaken Jairus's daughter from death and the woman comes behind Him. No doubt she made multiple attempts to touch His hem, but to no avail. She wasn't successful. But she continued pressing behind Him, and out of nowhere, her fountain of blood stopped immediately. Jesus paused and said, "Wait, somebody touched me."

Peter responds to Him and suggests that it is impossible to actually know who did the touching because of the massiveness of the crowd. However, Jesus emphasized, "Somebody touched me because virtue came out of me." And there she was, there, alone and bent over away from the massive crowd. She then opens up and confesses to Jesus what she had done. I definitely believe He stopped in His tracks for the woman to confess and give Him the glory for what has just transpired in her life. She is indeed made whole and she receives an additional benefit and that is she is now saved. She actually received a double portion of God's blessings because she was healed and was saved.

God is indeed a healer and restorer! When you allow Him to restore you, you've been restored. What was not working, God can cause to work; what was irrelevant, He can make relevant; what seemed irreversible, He can reverse; God is a *healer*! When you know the value of healing and restoration, you are ready to go on a journey, a pilgrimage, and a path called righteousness.

Divine Path

A shepherd is distinct from any leader. Their leadership skills come from God. They possess leadership skills that are second to none. Notice what David says about the leadership of his Shepherd. He mentions that His Shepherd does not make him do anything, coerce him, force him, demand him to; no, He leads him. Where does He lead him? He leads him to the path of righteousness.

This should be the common denominator for any persons in spiritual or secular leadership. The best way to lead is to guide. A great leader leads followers to do what's right and to experience what's beneficial. David suggests that his Shepherd leads him to a "path of righteousness." This is why I call it a divine path because the Shepherd will never lead us to a place of unrighteousness. He testifies that the Shepherd guides him to a place that's distinct, significant, and purposeful. God will never lead you into temptation nor does He tempts one to do evil (James 1:13–14). He leads us to the paths of righteousness.

Righteousness is a path that is purposeful, practical, and powerful. A godly leader leads persons to the place where God wants them and will use them. God always has His people heading in the right direction. He's a purposeful God and He has purposeful intentions for His creation. Just as shepherds have personal intentions for their sheep, so does the Lord for His flock. He wants to use you to full capacity. This is what shepherds do for their sheep: they lead, nurture, protect, and care for. God cares for us and one of the many ways of knowing He cares is knowing that He has a path designed, tailored, and customized only for us, and it's a path of righteousness.

The testament of any true leader is not to force or make anyone do anything. A true leader has no games, gimmicks, or schemes. No, they lead. They guide them. They guide them to a place of purpose and excellence. An effective leader guides with a practical purpose and a spirit of excellence and not manipulation. Peter gives sound advice on leading as an under-shepherd, with the dos and don'ts of successful shepherding ministry.

The passage 1 Peter 5:2–4 (NKJV) states, "Shepherd the flock of God which is among you, serving as overseers, not by compulsion but willingly, not for dishonest gain but eagerly; nor as being lords over those entrusted to you, but being examples to the flock; and when the Chief Shepherd appears, you will receive the crown of glory that does not fade away."

A shepherding leader is one who knows their purpose, and they don't go beyond their calling and anointing. Under-shepherds are not to be dishonest and know we are not to "lord" over anyone but simply to be examples to the flock as honest leaders. We are to lead with excellence and execution because our Chief Shepherd will appear one day to give us our unfading crown. The under-shepherd leads the sheep with shepherding care to guide them in their purpose. In like manner, God does the exact for us. He puts us into a place of destiny, purpose, and propel us to the next level of our lives because we have the right relationship and connection. What will get you to the next level of your life? It will be a certain path; in fact, a righteous one.

What's best for your destiny the Shepherd has provided for you? What direction do you need to go en route to your destiny? The right way. David testifies that his Shepherd has to lead him to the place of righteousness because of being on a path of righteousness. In order to be in a certain place and position in your life, it takes a specific process to get you there. Therefore, if you are going to pursue excellence, you must do it not on your terms but on the Shepherd's. Furthermore, He has ordained that His sheep must go down the righteous path because He will lead, guide, and direct them there.

When you are fulfilling God's purpose for your life, you can't do things as you please because doing so can easily put you on the wrong track, course, and path. This is why we need to be led.

I know you perhaps might be strong-headed and strong-willed. If so, you can end up doing your thing and not the Shepherd's agenda. It's good to be strong-minded and strong-willed, but it can also be dangerous. Trust me, you can end up on the path of wickedness instead of righteousness when things are done your way and not God's. Personal autonomy can be dangerous to play with. When we are truly led by the Shepherd, we allow Him to be in control, not ourselves.

This is why it is so important to allow God to lead us and we do not get in front of Him to lead. Shepherds lead because they know what's best for the sheep. God absolutely knows what's best for us and He knows what it takes to get us to the righteous path. David gives a powerful testimony about the paths of God, he says in Psalm 25:10 (NKJV), "All the paths of the LORD are mercy and truth. To such as keep His covenant and His testimonies. David understands the importance of being on the right side and path of destiny as opposed to the alternative."

David confesses in Psalm 31:3 (NKJV), "For You are my rock and my fortress; Therefore, for Your name's sake, Lead me and guide me. The tone of David's words in this text is, he needs the guidance of his Shepherd because if relying on his own guidance continually, he will indeed be lost. That's why he needed the guidance of God to take him to his rightful place. In order to get to your rightful place in life, you've got to follow the lead and direction of the Shepherd.

Many people have missed out on so many opportunities in their past simply because they had gotten in the way of God's lead. David recognizes the importance of letting God lead. He realizes that when God leads, He leads for His glory and He leads to guide. When we allow God to lead and guide our lives, He receives the glory. So then, there must be a purpose for the righteous path? I believe that God has His sheep on the path of righteousness for many reasons. I remember on my grandfather's farm; he had much land, and on what we called field number one, there was a fish pond. Over a period of time, we walked on the grass, wore down the grass, and to our surprise, with no blades or moving devices, we had made our own path.

While making the path, we walked in this specific pattern daily. And there it was—a path to the pond. However, I noticed as I have grown and became an adult, there was a reason why we walked in a certain direction and made the path with specific particulars. We made the path with curves and straight lines because we, first of all, wanted to avoid danger; we knew the terrain well and knew where to go and where to walk; in addition, there was another reason the path was made—to get us to our destination, the pond. I submit unto you, God's righteous path is for us to avoid danger, get to our destiny, and function in our blessings. This is why we let God lead because He has a reason for our paths in life.

Now on this path, God shows David another attribute of His name and character. David says, "He leadeth me in the paths of righteousness for His name's sake." On this righteous path, he has an encounter with *Jehovah–Tsidkenu* which means, "The Lord Our Righteousness." The Lord led David to the paths of righteousness because He, *Jehovah–Tsidkenu*, is righteous. Therefore, He will not lead His sheep to what's contrary to His character, integrity, and will.

When we are on the right path, we should observe the route while traveling on the divine path. He puts His sheep on this specific path for His name's sake, the Hebrew word sake translated ma'an means "so that, because of, for the sake of." This implies that our Shepherd puts us on this path of righteousness because of and the sake of His name. The Hebrew word he uses for the word name is šēm which is a masculine noun meaning a name and fame. It is what specifically identifies a person or anything. Jehovah–Tsidkenu is His name and it identifies who He is, God is righteous. Therefore, since God is righteous, He can only lead us through who He is, in His reputable character. He leads us to the paths of righteousness because of His righteousness and righteous reputation.

God's reputation cannot be compared too by anyone. He's God and God alone. However, through His characteristics of leading, guiding, and shepherding, He demonstrates certain qualities. He demonstrates guidance, grace, and goodness in His shepherding relationship with His sheep.

Guidance

No one can guide like God. God guides the sheep and His true sheep will follow. By nature, sheep will follow who are considered to be the leader. Therefore, His sheep will follow Him because they know their Shepherd. Jesus in John's gospel records these words and uses a perfect illustration about shepherding:

John 10:1–5 (NKJV):

> Most assuredly, I say to you, he who does not enter the sheepfold by the door, but climbs up some other way, the same is a thief and a robber. But he who enters by the door is the shepherd of the sheep. To him, the doorkeeper opens, and the sheep hear his voice, and he calls his own sheep by name and leads them out. And when he brings out his own sheep, he goes before them; and the sheep follow him, for they know his voice. Yet they will by no means follow a stranger, but will flee from him, for they do not know the voice of strangers.

Jesus gives the epitome of true shepherding. He firmly says that true shepherds are not robbers. He adds true shepherds enter in the correct way to shepherd. In addition, His sheep know His voice and He calls their name and leads them. The way they follow is because they know His voice. *Voice* in the Greek is *phone* which means "tone." The Shepherd has a certain sound and the sheep know that distinct sound and will follow.

Grace

God gives grace to the sheep as an act of benevolence. He doesn't have to lead sheep, but He chooses to. That's grace. He gives them nourishment, provision, and Shepherding care because He cares for the sheep unconditionally. Just as earthly shepherds have grace upon their sheep, so does the Lord toward His sheep. There's an awesome illustration of the shepherd's grace when sheep are sick: the earthly shepherd doesn't leave them out in the pasture for time to heal them on their own. No, the shepherd begins to show the sick sheep grace to restore it back to a proper standard of health.

As I stated earlier, I had the privilege to visit a sheep farm to study sheep and gather information, and the shepherdess shared something with me that was vitally enlightening. She informed me that a true shepherd/shepherdess has tremendous compassion for their flock, and when they are sick, they give them the proper care they need for restoration. She also shared with me that a shepherd/shepherdess looks at the flock as though they are helpless and they need consistent care from their shepherd/shepherdess. She also shared with me that a true shepherd/shepherdess does not own sheep just to have them in their possession. No, the shepherd sheep because they have a passion to care for them. She also lectured about how important it was for the shepherd/shepherdess to provide the essentials for the flock because they cannot produce them themselves.

I was also informed by the shepherdess that sheep need leading for a variety of reasons because there are some things they cannot do. Therefore, the shepherd/shepherdess is there to give them grace as well. For instance, when they are sick, the shepherd gives them medication when they are preyed upon by the beast of the field, the shepherd gives them protection, and when they are led to a lush field, they encounter the provision of the shepherd. In parallel, God has grace upon His sheepfold and gives them shepherding care to restore and put on the righteous path.

Goodness

The psalmist declares how the Lord has led him into a tranquil state and he experiences the goodness of the Lord while in the path of righteousness. What constitutes the goodness of God? When David can declare that his needs are met, he's in a place of tranquility and restoration, his soul is healed, and he's been led in a righteous path. He's experiencing the goodness of God.

Therefore, all of us can certainly attest that God has been good. When you can see the favor of God on your life, live in abundance of His blessings, experiencing peace, you've experienced personal revival and given protection. That's the goodness of God.

When you know that you have overcome overwhelming situations, you can thank God for His goodness. Life is filled with many struggles and multiple moments of discouragement, but when you've been delivered and set free, you can be thankful for the goodness of God. God has many blessings for you. Also, He has blessed us in the past. Therefore, when we know that if He has taken care of us in the past, He can repeat the process and give you what you need and more. For the sake of His name He gives us guidance, grace, and goodness.

While experiencing tranquility and peace, things are lovely, calm, and blissful. However, things do change; the reality is life does have moments when peace seems to have been transformed into problems. Also, the problems we face in this pilgrimage called life can cause us to accept defeat and not try to overcome the problems we encounter. This type of thinking we do not need. However, we need to have what I call an attitude adjustment and shift our focus, not on our problems, but we should focus on our God.

Therefore, when we focus on the problems life presents to us, and not the goodness of God, we do not give glory to Him. When you dwell on your situations rather than the goodness of God, we do not revere Him in the correct way He deserves. Paul gives great advice when he wrote to the Philippian church in Philippians 4:8 (NKJV), "Finally, brethren, whatever things are true, whatever things are noble, whatever things are just, whatever things are pure, whatever things are lovely, whatever things are of good report, if there is any virtue and if there is anything praiseworthy—meditate on these things." God is good and we must thank Him for His goodness and think about things that will not discourage nor destroy us.

When we think about things such as Paul refers, it gives us peace rather than pain; therefore, we can focus on the goodness of God more, as opposed to the negative things life has. God is so good to us that He goes to the ultimate level of grace and has our best interest at heart. The psalmist's glory to God in an exhortation of praise in Psalm 100:5 (NKJV), "For the LORD is good; His mercy is everlasting, And His truth endures to all generations." The word good *tôb*: is an adjective which means "good, well-pleasing, fruitful, morally correct, proper, and convenient." Therefore, we as sheep must recognize that the goodness of our Shepherd endures to all generations and we actually experience His goodness because He is well pleasing, He's fruitful, He's morally correct (holy), nothing incorrect, and He's proper and certainly convenient. Nahum puts it this way, "The LORD is good, A stronghold in the day of trouble; And He knows those who trust in Him" (Nah. 1:7, NKJV).

We cannot deny that God is good. He's good to all and He knows how to take care of us. Our Shepherd is good to all of us and He renders to us what we need for this pilgrimage called life, and He extends His compassionate grace to give us sustenance.

We should be thankful because of the goodness of our God. God does not have to be good to us, but I'm grateful He is. In His goodness, we have a plethora of benefits, and we should be thankful and bless His name. The psalmist says this in Psalm 103:1–2 (NKJV), "Bless the LORD, O my soul; And all that is within me, bless His holy name! Bless the LORD, O my soul, And forget not all His benefits." We should never forget how the Lord benefits us. The way the psalmist suggests our way of showing our greatness to God by not forgetting His benefits is to bless Him! We have so many reasons to be thankful for His goodness because there are many things we don't deserve but He still gives. God blesses us in so many capacities, and we should be thankful for His goodness because He often blesses us more than we deserve. We should bless Him continuously and consistently because of His goodness; in fact, we should give our all in blessing Him with our soul. Therefore, on our pilgrimage on earth, we need God's guidance, grace, and goodness on the path of righteousness.

We must know He has us on the path of righteousness, not wickedness. There's a difference. The two paths lead to different destinations. When I visited the sheep farm, the shepherdess shared something else with me that blessed me in preacher's words homiletically. She stated, "true shepherds have the best intent for the sheep and they will do nothing wrong to lead them astray." Beloved, you must be extremely careful of who leads and feed you. Also, you must be careful of your associations.

One reality of life is we are known by the company we keep. In fact, when led on the path of righteousness, there will be wicked lures trying to get you to get off of your route of righteousness. To name no one better, David knows what can be done by sheep when not on the path of righteousness. He knows that there can be wicked behavior when there is no conviction nor direction in our lives. Therefore, it is imperative that we seek after a righteous path because there's a predator lurking with certain lures, trying

42

to get us to get off of the path of righteousness and wander us on the wicked path.

We can never underestimate the power of influence when we are trying to live lives of holiness and righteousness. There's a predator who will try his best to get us off this path, but we must be aware of his devices, plots, and schemes. Listen to what Paul says to the church at Corinth in his first epistle in 1 Corinthians 15:33 (KJV), "Be not deceived: evil communications corrupt good manners." We must be extremely careful of our surroundings because corruption can infect anyone. There must be an inner strength within us to convict us to be led in the right direction and not be evilly influenced to get off course with the Shepherd.

My friends, when things are going well, blissful, and you're in the Shepherd's care, understand that sooner or later, adversity will come. The hymn writer suggests in the lyrics of the classic "Hold to God's Unchanging Hand," that "life is filled with swift transition." Although sheep are under the shepherd's care, it still does not prevent problems and predators. When there is a season of tranquility and cud chewing (a peaceful daze) be aware because on the horizon, there it is, adversity coming within the flock. In fact, it's dark, it's cold, also there's a valley and death seems to be close to being a shadow away. Although while in this valley, the Shepherd guards His sheep and protects them carefully.

Part Two

He Guards Us

Yea, though I walk through the valley of the shadow of death, I will fear no evil; For You are with me; Your rod and Your staff, they comfort me.

You prepare a table before me in the presence of my enemies; You anoint my head with oil; My cup runs over.

—Psalm 23:4-5

With this provisional need, the Shepherd provides the sheep emotional and earthly needs. In the central verse of this psalm, David testifies to the Shepherd about his condition, calamity, and comfort. After being led to a place of purpose and pleasure, now he's being led to a place of pain. David honestly declares something about his condition when he says, "I walk through." He has a condition and it is not a pleasant one. David is not alone. We, too, have some conditions in our lives that cause us pain.

He also states that he's in a state of calamity. There are, in fact, times when we are at a loss in certain seasons of our lives. We have lost some things and might I say some things need to be lost and others gained. Honestly, when we encounter a season of loss, it doesn't feel good. In fact, it feels horrible. Calamity is a part of life that many of us do not like to deal with it, but it is the reality. Actually, calamity can put us in a dark place, and if we are not careful, it can have further repercussions that can be dangerous to our mental well-being. There's something within us that is agitated when we lose something. In this valley, the psalmist actually feels at a loss. But there's good news. While in this valley, he's not alone; he has comfort.

David gladly confesses that his Shepherd is with him in this season of difficulty, discouragement, and seemingly near death. With all the calamitous circumstances we have in life, we should be encouraged that our Shepherd has not left us in the valley alone. He's there with us in our valleys. He gives us comfort in our valleys, by knowing that what we encounter in our valleys although they may be challenging, gives us hope in knowing He's with us. Yes, even when death is near, He's with us! That's the confirmation every believer wants to know: "You are with us."

After studying this psalm from various perspectives, I've learned that a shepherd is not only a provisionary and guide, they also guard. When you think about a true shepherd from a perspective of a job description, in their character, they are protectors of their flock. As I stated earlier, a true shepherd and shepherdess will always have a passion to provide and protect their flock. When I went to the sheep farm, the shepherdess shared with me that "shepherds and shepherdesses who are true will always be protective of their flock."

David gives a personal testimony about His shepherd and unveils that his shepherd is a protector.

Shepherds have a great passion to protect the sheep because they understand that sheep go through difficult experiences. Experiencing difficulty in life is, in fact, a valley. Life is filled with moments which are not easy to endure. Life can get very discouraging, dark, and difficult; no, life is not easy. Life presents many difficult moments, and if we're not careful, it can damage and destroy us. All of us encounter valley moments, and if we are honest, these moments can overwhelm us. When you receive a pink slip from your employer, that's a valley; when your home is foreclosed, that's a valley; when your vehicle is repossessed, that's a valley; experiencing sickness is a valley; the loss of a loved one is a valley. People encounter valleys daily. In fact, the valleys we face can become very tough to deal with. To make matters worse, it seems like some of the valleys become deeper when we go through a series of struggles, but the good news is this causes us to depend on the protection of God.

The valleys we face in life can be downright depressing if we allow the troubles that accompany it to overwhelm us. The troubles we face in life are, in fact, difficult; therefore, we must depend on the Shepherd to give us protection. We certainly need the protection of the Shepherd because life can give some heavy blows at times and the protection of the Shepherd gives us tranquility and security.

One thing about shepherds is they actually love valleys because of the water sufficiency the valley gives. The valley also has great greens. Shepherds love to lead their sheep to the valleys because of its resources. However, the valley has conveniences that are beneficial for the sheep; however it also inconveniences. The conveniences of the valley are the green grass and the supply of water. Although, the inconveniences are the existence of predators. While the shepherd leads the flock through the valley, there's something that's so near to them that's dark, dismal, and discouraging, and it can have permanent implications.

The Facts about the Valley

Unavoidable

The valleys we face are unavoidable. No matter who you are, what you do, you cannot avoid the valley. There will be an experience of the valley by those who love God and they cannot escape it. It's just something we must go through. Life will not be easy at all times; there will be some rough roads and rocky journeys that we must encounter. Some parishioners even think that under-shepherds don't go through as much as them. No, pastors can't avoid the valley experience, they (we) go through many valleys. Some even believe that when a person gives their life to the Lord, "all of my troubles will be over." Now I must admit, that sounds good, but it's not true.

Transparently speaking, just because you've accepted Christ in your life doesn't mean that you will not go through valley moments. My friends, even with Christ on board you will still go through storms. This actually reminds me of the narrative of the disciples on the sea when it was raging. The account of Mark's gospel gives the actuality of going through a storm even with Christ on board.

> On the same day, when evening had come, He said to them, "Let us cross over to the other side."

> Now when they had left the multitude, they took Him along in the boat as He was. And other little boats were also with Him.

> And a great windstorm arose, and the waves beat into the boat, so that it was already filling.

> But He was in the stern, asleep on a pillow. And they awoke Him and said to Him, "Teacher, do You not care that we are perishing?" (Mk 4:35–38, NKJV)

What blesses me in this lesson is, Jesus gives the disciples a command to go to the other side. While they are sailing to their destination, a confrontation challenges them. They are fearful and they believe that death is ever so close . . . they are frantic and they wake Jesus up—He was sleeping—and ask, Does He care that they were perishing? What blessed me in the text was they should have never assumed they were the only ones experiencing the storm because the text says there were also other little boats alongside Him. My friends, never assume you are the only one going through some type of adversity or difficulty because the reality is all of us go through difficulties. However, when you read the text, it also says that Jesus was on board; so then, never assume because Christ is your Lord and Savior that you will never encounter difficulties because the reality is, you will. Make no mistake about it: our valleys are unavoidable.

Although, they were in a storm with Christ on board. The storm did not destroy them because Christ stood and rebuked the winds and there was a great calm. Have you been through something and it caused you to be curious about your survival? Just as the disciples, we find ourselves in moments of curiosity and inquisitiveness. They asked Christ a question and He gave the answer. He not only said to "peace to be still" but He also showed the disciples He cared about them and their stressful circumstance. In like manner, He shows us there's nothing we can through that can get Him away from His care for us. Therefore, when we go through moments of peril and pain, we must know that our Shepherd cares for us with shepherding care. Although we face circumstances that are unavoidable, the Savior's care for us takes us through.

Unpleasant

The valleys of life are not pleasant. They are, in fact, unpleasant. When you have encountered so much toil in your valley, it gives no pleasure, it gives pain. Life has many painful moments, and if we could avoid and escape them, we would. They are unavoidable and certainly unpleasant. Although life has moments of pleasure, it also has its share of pain. Therefore, it's difficult to appreciate your journey when you've always experienced pleasure and never pain. Pain is a part of your journey, and it can leave one feeling down, depressed, and not expect deliverance. Actually, it's hard to get to the top of the mountain if you're in the valley. When you give your absolute best and still end up short of your goals, that's painful and definitely discouraging. When you see other individuals who seem to care less but still seem to have some level of success, that's confusing as well. While going through the mill of life's problems and perils, it can be very painful.

When you are not at peace, it is not a pleasant feeling. There are so many are not feeling pleasure in life, and when they experience, pleasure can be dangerous to the body. No one really wants to go through times of oddity. When things are not in pleasant posture, things become odd. Therefore, when things are odd, they transition into abnormality 60 and this will be problematic because what was known as pleasurable is now unpleasant. Experiencing unpleasant valleys can cause health problems, yes, the exterior (valleys and problems) can affect your interior.

Sometimes when the unpleasantness of life overwhelms us, we must understand that the valley is not permanent but temporary. Paul mentions something about experiencing trials and their temporary timespan. The passage 2 Corinthians 4:18 (NKJV), "While we do not look at the things which are seen, but at the things which are not seen. For the things which are seen are temporary, but the things which are not seen are eternal."

Therefore, in your season of valley unpleasantness, remember that it will not last forever. Remember that whatever you encounter, your Shepherd will help you survive and take you through your valleys by His grace.

Unpredictable

Life is not only associated with unpleasant realities, there are also unpredictable moments in life as well. One thing is for sure, life is filled with valley experiences that are certainly unpredictable. The swift transitions of life can hit us at any given moment. The valleys we go through in life can and will come unannounced and unwelcomed. When the valleys come, they don't notify us by mail, email, tweets, or Facebook that they are coming. No, they come unpredictably.

The author of Ecclesiastes confirms the unpredictability of life in Ecclesiastes 9:11–12 (NKJV):

> I returned and saw under the sun that—The race is not to the swift, nor the battle to the strong, nor bread to the wise, nor riches to men of understanding, nor favor to men of skill; But time and chance happen to them all. For man also does not know his time: Like fish taken in a cruel net, like birds caught in a snare, so the sons of men are snared in an evil time, when it falls suddenly upon them.

Life is unpredictable. We make plans and at times we make them days, weeks, and even months in advance. However, the reality is we don't know what can happen at any given moment. The valleys can come while the sun is shining on a beautiful day where no clouds are in sight; the birds are singing with joy, and before you know it, the unpredictability of life has come to your residence without your approval or your awareness.

Although the valleys are unpredictable, what makes them bearable is knowing that the Shepherd is with you. In fact, He's leading you. With predators observing sheep in the valley, they still are in a tranquil state only because of the presence of their shepherd. So then, we should not be dismayed even when unpredictability has invaded our vicinity because we have our Shepherd!

When we have unexpected things happen to us (might I admit they can be very oppressive), we have hope because He's with us. Life's unpredictability is real. In fact, when you felt wonderful physically and went to the doctor only to receive news from your doctor that there's something abnormal. You've been employed for years and went to work one morning only to discover that you are no longer employed. While walking, you decided to go to your mailbox, and there it is, a letter that has turned your day upside down.

Therefore, we are surrounded with unpredictability, but the sheep of God's pasture should be encouraged only because of the presence of the Shepherd. To that end, we must know God's availability can handle life's unpredictability.

Untimely

The valleys of life are not just unavoidable, unpleasant, and unpredictable. They are also untimely. The valleys of life just seem to come at the wrong time. It seems when things are going good and you feel the comfort of being in the presence of the Shepherd, and then all of a sudden, here it comes—trouble. Yes, coming supposedly at the wrong time. However, not only could things be going good, things can also be going bad and more untimely challenges can be added. This certainly is not easy to endure, but sometimes untimely things are necessary.

Sometimes, personally, you may think the timing could be wrong, and at times you wonder how much more adversity you actually can take. When you experience one obstacle after the next and there never seems to be an end, trust your Shepherd. Sheep by nature have untimely circumstances that happen to them, but their shepherd is there to support them. Therefore, when we go through the untimely episodes of life, we must still be content in our relationship with God and continually trust Him despite the difficulty.

The proverbial writer suggested something about bad timing in Proverbs 27:14 (NKJV), "He who blesses his friend with a loud voice, rising early in the morning, it will be counted a curse to him." Solomon says that sometimes a blessing can actually seem like a curse, especially when the timing is wrong.

Sometimes timing can be devastating. We often find ourselves in seasons of bad timing. In fact, the valleys of life can seem so dark, dismal, and deep that it makes bad timing seem worse. It also feels like hope has disappeared, but when the Shepherd is with you, there's hope. With all the untimely misfortunes we face, I believe there's a purpose behind it and the Shepherd will take care of you while going through it. Therefore, hold on and trust the Shepherd, because He's with you. A factual reality about the valley is it has good points to experience as well as bad. Although untimely experiences may not seem beneficial at the moment, a lesson should be learned while enduring the adversity. That is, you are surviving the untimely moments of life because of the sustaining power of the Shepherd. Moreover, this should be the encouraging factor in your life when the untimely moments of the valley are being experienced.

Untimely moments are unpredictable and so are predators. While in the presence of the shepherd, sheep have to deal with the untimely reality of predators. Now, the reality of predators in green pastures is one thing, but experiencing them in the valley is another. Although with the arsenal of bad experiences in the valley, what gives tremendous hope is knowing that He guards us with certain things.

Divine Presence

Shepherds in the east led their sheep into rough terrain, through dangerous spots, and sheer cliffs as they protected them with their presence through the journey of the valley. Although dark and uncertain, they trust the leading of the shepherd to take them to a place of comfort and peace, even in the valley.In order for protection to be given, there has to be some type of discomfort for those who need security. For one thing for sure about sheep—they are prey animals. Predators observe them often. In fact, predators are so aggressive, they'd even try to invade the flock while knowing the shepherd is present. They have a zealous ambition to interfere and cause devastation among the flock; they'll even go to the full extent trying to harm or kill.

However, there's no need to worry because the shepherd is present while in the vicinity of the valley. Although predators come, the shepherd is still there to validate his presence to assure the flock he will protect them. The presence of the shepherd is certainly needed by sheep when the valley is dark and looks identical to death. The habitat of the valley and the shadow of death is threatening. Something interesting about the "the valley of the shadow of death," ṣalmāwet is a masculine noun meaning "a death shadow, a deep shadow, and darkness." Some declare this as the darkness of death. For we know there is much darkness and evil around us and we need God's help to endure. The presence of the Shepherd is needed because there's darkness all around. When times are dark and discouraging in the valley, having the presence of the shepherd makes it better. When you are in a dangerous place and cannot see clearly, knowing the shepherd is near brings about a great calm. There's nothing like being in a dangerous place with having His divine presence.

This place of danger and death is so suspect because where there's darkness, there's evil. Despite how people try to deny it, evil is a reality. It is the opposite of holiness and David understands this darkness is a symbolic state of evil. The word evil is referred to as "moral or ethical failure." The Complete Word Study Bible shares this concept about evil by explaining this noun, "The word indicates realities that are inherently evil, wicked, or bad; the psalmist feared no evil (Ps. 23:4)." The noun also depicts people of wickedness, that is, "wicked people." It is certainly dangerous when you are in a dark place with demonic people. There will be spiritual warfare to those who earnestly desire the Shepherd's lead. While the Shepherd leads, the forces of evil will try to invade and conquer the sheep but the Shepherd's presence gives sheep the encouragement to trust in their Shepherd's care.

When facing moments of darkness, it's good to have the presence of the Shepherd because He's there to protect us. David is absolutely confident in the presence of his Shepherd. He speaks with no uncertainty or doubt; he firmly declares that his Shepherd is with him.

David is in a dark place in his life, and he's not spiritually intoxicated to realize this fact. David is in a dark place; he's in a setting that actually feels like death. He honestly confesses he's in a valley and death seems like a literal shadow. Now, he didn't say he was in the valley of death, but he does state the valley with death's shadow. This indicates that David is experiencing some dark moments. He's certainly no stranger to dark moments, and many times, he ran for his life to escape those dark moments because of fear.

David was afraid on many occasions. He fled from Saul; also, he fled from his son, Absalom. David had many fearful moments, and if you are honest, you do as well. When you are in an environment and it actually feels like death, that can be fearful. David is not like many of the super-sized saints of the day. He doesn't imply that he's not going to claim this valley experience; he doesn't suggest that this encounter is not real. No, he acknowledges he's in a valley and the actual experience is so horrific it feels like death is so near.

As stated earlier, sheep do not have the best vision and they are afraid at night, especially under new circumstances. They are fidgety and scared; and sometimes, when shepherds would lead their sheep into the valley, they would become afraid because the depth of the valley could actually block the sun. Therefore, when the sun was blocked, the sheep would be afraid because of the absence of light. We, too, are like that at times. Honestly, it's just something about the dark. Even the disciples were afraid of the dark while Jesus walked on the water to them. Being afraid in dark hours is common; you'd be afraid, too, if you saw someone walking on the sea when it's dark, especially the fourth watch of the night.

Sheep were extremely afraid in the dark due to the reality of predators. David says he has an unpleasant feeling, and this feeling feels like death. There are many who feel like giving up because of their emotional exhaustion; they are tired of the valley. Yes, tired of discouraging times, financial pressure, health concerns, low self-esteem, and etc. Conversely, catch what David says: he says that he is walking through the valley of the shadow of death, which means he does not have to experience this horrifying episode forever because he's only walking through. Therefore, this is not a permanent experience although it's necessary. Sometimes, we go through the valleys of life because God is not trying to detour us from difficulties, but rather develop as disciples with the difficulties.

When you honestly access your relationship with the Shepherd, should you be in spiritual denial or unethical exegesis of God's Word? I firmly believe you should take life for what it is and have exegetical integrity, meanwhile having faith in the Shepherd and believing that He can deliver you from your fears. Often, some become so discouraged in the process of the valley they actually give up. Some people are on the verge of giving up in life. No, continue to walk through the valley one step at a time. Also, one day at a time until you exit it.

Consequently, they feel that life is not worth living due to the perplexing pains of the valley. Don't surrender because you are having a suffering season. No, continue to allow the Shepherd to lead you through the valley, and eventually, you'll see the sun again because you're being led by the Shepherd.

While walking through this passing near Death Valley experience, the psalmist also has an encounter with evil. Therefore, while in this vicinity of death's shadow, evil is ever so close. In fact, while this experience is dark and depressing, there's hope because the Shepherd is in the valley experience with him. In like manner, just as the Shepherd was with David, He's with us as well. Isn't it good to know that you and I are not in our struggle alone? Our Shepherd is with us. Whether it's in green pastures or the valley of death's shadow. Yes, He the Shepherd will be with us continually. He's with you in comfort and chaos; He's with you in blessings and burdens. He will render His shepherding care for you despite your environment or experience.

Trouble is so near to David that he calls it the shadow of death. How close can you get than a shadow? Although the shadow is not death itself, he feels like it is so close. In fact, David feels like death is nothing but a shadow away, and ever so close to him. Sometimes, we have so many close calls and the circumstances experienced was so severe and possibly fatal that we understand that death was so near. When we are in a certain context such as this, we must remember that the shepherd is there for his sheep. Therefore, when you are in a valley experience, you must understand that God is testing you to bring out the best in you.

Protecting sheep is what the shepherd's call of duty is. The shepherd has the intellect and instinct to protect the flock. Although being deep in the valley of the shadow of death has many challenges, the shepherd is there to provide security for the sheep. In the same manner, God takes care of the sheep of His pasture. He takes care of us, even while we go through near-death experiences and encounter evil. Indeed, when we go through challenging experiences, we must never forget our Shepherd because He's there for us to protect, provide, and give peace. Therefore, when you go through a near-death encounter and the presence of evil is all around you, you don't have to worry about temporary circumstances because the Shepherd is giving a great measure of His permanent providence to protect you.

My friend, evil is not mythological, it's factual. Evil is all around us. It has power over those who succumb to it. The world is filled with evil, and it has a way of destroying persons from their intended purpose with God. As we observe the world, we would discover that this world is in bad condition and it is in need of the Shepherd's care.

The presence of evil is prevalent in the world and is making a major impact on it. The world is full of much trouble, strife, contention, immorality, and so much more. David confesses he is in the valley of the shadow of death; he also acknowledges that evil is closely around him. While surrounded by the very presence of evil, he does not fear because he is accompanied by his Shepherd. Therefore, when we think about the conditions of the world, we must not fear because the Shepherd is with us to do what we can't.

Do your valleys causes you to experience fear? I'm sure they do. However, what makes the difference? The presence of the shepherd. Sheep were very frightened by the dark valleys and it gave them a feeling of discomfort, and David mentions that the discomforting feeling of sheep is evil. When you are in an environment that causes extreme discomfort and it is contrary to the will of God, my friend, that's evil. The remedy for evil is Jesus Christ! This world needs a Savior! When sheep are in a hostile environment, they become fearful and rely on the shepherd. Sheep have to deal with the unavoidable, unpleasant, unpredictable, and untimely realities.

Although predators are within the valley the Shepherd's presence gives a great calm to the sheep. When you think about your life and the adversity you've encountered in the valley, adding predators to the list causes more tension. You could even feel the evil tension in the atmosphere, but because you know the Shepherd is with you, it makes the difference. Therefore, when the predators come, the Shepherd will be prepared for them and have peace within the flock.

While going through the valleys of life, it can mess with your emotions. Going through many struggles can have an effect on you emotionally and eventually damage your spirituality. When you are in a dark situation and have ferocious predators around you, it can be certainly stressful. They are pursuing you from all directions and trying to destroy you at your most vulnerable point. You feel like destruction is ever so close, and you need the presence of your Shepherd to see you through this perplexing process.

When you are going through circumstances that seem so depressing and dark, the best alternative to turn to is the divine. Just as sheep in nature need their shepherd, in like manner, disciples of Christ need their Good Shepherd as well. We need our Good Shepherd to protect us in the valleys of life because the valleys of life can be very unkind, unpleasant, and unforgiving and even cause death.

It's imperative to know that the Shepherd will secure you in your valley experiences. Although, the experiences life presents to us can be troubling and difficult to process, however, when the shepherd is with his sheep they feel at peace, knowing their protector is with them. In fact, you should feel the same way. When you have the God of the universe protecting and providing for you even in tough spaces and places, you should have confidence just because He's there!

Currently, in this postmodern age with the fast-paced society and instant influence we live in, we must still trust the Shepherd.

Additionally, we should be encouraged because if David had the benefits of the Shepherd, then we, too, have them as well. Therefore, be inspired because although David experienced God's provisions centuries ago, we must remember that God is eternal and what He has done for David He can also do for you and I. It's not too late; He still provides not only resources but Himself also.

Are you thankful for His presence? You should be. Unfortunately, some have issues of disbelief when it comes to the presence, provision, and power of God. However, those who believe recognize and acknowledge His presence. David has no doubt that his Shepherd is with him in his valley. Just as David has confidence in his Shepherd's presence, so should you. You should trust and believe that God is with you despite your struggles.

David recognizes *Jehovah–Shammah* (The Lord is present) is with him because he declares, "You are with me." *Yahweh–Shammah* is referenced in Ezekiel 48:35 (KJV) It was round about eighteen thousand measures: and the name of the city from that day shall be, The LORD is there." Do you know that the Lord is there? He's there all the time. He's there while you are reading these words. Continue to trust Him.

Divine Protection

David confesses how his Shepherd is with him, His rod and staff. Understanding these two instruments shepherds use is very important. There are some things we need that are necessary for life, that is, we need discipline, correction, and protection. These things are so vitally important to possess because these necessities are needed with our relationship with God. If there's something we need to attain our purposeful plight with our Shepherd, it's certainly these three necessities.

Discipline used by shepherds as they protected their sheep was indeed crucial. The rod was often worn at the belt of shepherds; it was also used by shepherds for different reasons. One to mention was disciplinary reasons. Shepherds would use the rod to discipline or correct the sheep when they needed correction. In every flock, there are sheep who are stubborn and selfish, and at times, need to be disciplined due to their rebellious behavior. Stubborn sheep have a propensity to stray from the shepherd's care and wander to other pastures. Often, when sheep became stubborn, the shepherd would use the rod to break their legs to discipline them. In addition, the shepherd would also use a special substance to make a cast and place around the sheep leg to heal their brokenness.

There are, in fact, times when we need to be disciplined, and sometimes, the shepherd has to give us disciplinary action to correct us for our unethical conduct. Have you ever been disciplined by God? I'm sure you have. If not, keep living and you will experience His discipline. There are times when we will be disciplined by God, and sometimes, He has to chastise us to get us back to our rightful place with Him. It has been said, when the shepherd gives sheep discipline, they become more attached to the shepherd. Therefore, if we are not careful, we can easily be detached from the flock. So God has to give us the discipline to signify His concern for us when we stray. There are times when we need to be corrected by God, and when He reproves us, it shows His love for us. The psalmist stated this fact in Psalm 94:10 (KJV), "He that chastiseth the heathen, shall not he correct? He that teacheth man knowledge, shall not he know? The shepherd corrects the sheep because he knows what's best for the flock. He gives us His love and He wants us to understand that His discipline is given for correction and instruction.

The rod is also given for protecting the sheep. The shepherd would not use the rod for correctional purposes or by means of discipline when the sheep had predators in their surroundings. The shepherd would use the rod to keep predators away from harming the sheep and even possibly killing them. Therefore, when predators would approach the flock, the shepherd would notify them that they were not welcomed simply by using his rod. For instance, when predators came to the flock out of the brush, the shepherd would throw it at times to let them know their presence is not welcomed. When the shepherd would throw the rod, the predators would normally run away because of the awareness of the protective presence of the shepherd.

The rod of the shepherd is actually powerful. When something four feet in length can keep away predators and actually keep the sheep in line with the shepherd as well, that's powerful. God uses His rod to keep us in line with His purpose for our lives and also to keep predators and enemies at bay with us. The rod is given to protect you from your adversary, Satan. Satan wants to destroy you, but He's limited in his ways of destruction because the Lord has His rod in your life. Satan wants to destroy your purpose and indwell you with wickedness. Therefore, he can't destroy you in the valley of darkness and death because of the rod the Shepherd has put in your life.

The influence of Satan is real, but the rod of the Shepherd is there to smash and demolish his wicked influence. Satan has to keep his hands off of you when the rod is evident in your life. Although, he will make multiple attempts to revisit you and lure you into his snares, but allow the Shepherd to implement the rod in your life so that you can see His protection and provision. Are you thankful for your rod of discipline, correction, and protection that your Shepherd gives you? David is certainly thankful for the rod because he understands that the presence of the Shepherd is paramount in his life. He also recognizes that his comfort has come by means of what the Shepherd has constituted in his life, His rod and staff. Why do you appreciate discipline? The rod. Why do you value correction and instruction? The rod. Why do you express gratitude for protection and provision? The rod.

The rod is a very intricate part of the life of a believer in Christ. Therefore, when we go through a process of discipline, correction, and instruction, it's for our betterment, not our detriment. So, the shepherd provides this part of the process to teach us vital lessons on correction and discipline when we need it. It's also to give us protection when predators approach us. David testifies that the presence of the Shepherd comes through His rod and staff because when you've experienced both of them, you will have comfort.

The shepherd also has an instrument called a staff. The staff is designed for protection. It is also a symbol of the grace of God. The grace of God is essential to all, especially those who know they don't deserve it. When God gives grace, we must understand that He doesn't have to do so, He chooses to.

Therefore, when we understand that by His choosing He gives grace, we should be humbled. The Shepherd gives His grace to His sheep, and while doing so, we should never devalue it. However, we should be grateful for it.

Like the rod is a symbol or representation of God's authority, in addition, the staff is a symbol or representation of the grace of God. Just as He demonstrates His authority to stubborn sheep and predators, He also demonstrates the compassion of His character by applying the staff in our lives to give us sufficient grace. We absolutely need the staff! It is something God uses in our daily walk with Him that is definitely realized in the moments of darkness, danger, and drowning.

Darkness in the Valley

The child of God certainly experiences dark days. As I stated prior, some conclude when they come to Christ their troubles will be over. However, that's not true. In the east, sheep would experience fearful moments, especially when the sun was not shining. So, while in the valleys, they would go through moments when they assumed it was dark because there are certain places in the valley where the sun doesn't shine and they become very timid in the dark. Therefore, when they assume it's dark, they see a shadow; in fact, shadows are very close to them and this frightens them. David utters the words, "The valley of the shadow of death," basically because of its darkness.

We don't have to have fear of death because Christ has taken its sting away (1 Cor. 15:55). Therefore, if death has no sting, the grave has no victory. This is indicative because of the work of Christ's death, burial, and resurrection from the grave with all power in His possession. So, we do not have to be afraid of death because Christ defeated it. With that being said, don't pretend that you never have dark moments in your life because you do. Furthermore, darkness is a difficult thing to deal with and we encounter it often. Therefore, how do we get out of it? By following the Shepherd, because He will eventually lead us to a place where the sun shines again. In fact, we encounter dark moments spiritually; however, there's hope in those seasons we encounter "dark valley spiritual moments." Therefore, what's the solution when we are in spiritual darkness? The Son of God! Just as the sun gives light in the natural, the Son gives light in the spiritual. Although we encounter dark moments at times spiritually, our hope is in Jesus Christ. He's the only one who can conquer fear in our lives.

Danger in the Valley

Not only is the valley dark, it's also dangerous. With the darkness that dwells in the valley, there are also dangerous parts of the valley and some parts are extremely dangerous. The danger that surrounds the flock is not only when it's dark, but when there are predators in the dark. The wolves and the hyenas can smell where the flock is located in the valley and best believe they are coming. To add, they come not alone but in packs. Have you ever encountered moments like that where there wasn't one thing that came at you; however, it was many things that came at you at one specific time?

The valley is dangerous and dark and this negative combination often leads to discouragement. It's very easy to be discouraged when you are in a discouraging place at a discouraging time. However, don't allow fear to intimidate you. Why? Because of the Shepherd and His staff. If it were not for the grace of God, you very well could have been left alone in the valley. But He is there with us in the dark. Just the fact He loves you and cares should encourage you to go on believing you can make it out of this place of darkness and danger. He protects you with His rod and staff at all times.

Do you deserve His staff in your life? For sure we know some things we do not deserve but He still gives us. When wolves come to us and we can live to tell about how He's taken care of us in the midst of an attack, that's grace. When you've been blessed beyond what you deserve, that's grace. When your enemies could only get so close to you because the Shepherd was protecting you with His rod and staff, that's grace. Grace is something God gives us, and as recipients of His bestowed grace, we should be thankful. The Lord has graced us with favor and the staff of the Shepherd directs us to the places He has designed for our lives. Therefore, danger of the valley is real, but we must know that our Shepherd is real as well and He will see to it that we are protected providentially while experiencing the valley of life.

When those who are led have a leader, and they know their leader is a protector, provider, and also a producer of grace.

Drowning in the Ravine

The shepherd would also grant grace to the sheep in times of drowning. Sheep would sometimes get into the rivers and ravine and because of the density of their wool, they would often drown. However, the shepherd would rescue them in the river or ravine because of his staff. He would stoop down from the riverbank and extend the staff around the neck of the sheep and pull it to safety. Many of us can relate to the staffing grace of God as He rescued us with His staff. Yes, there's deliverance in the staff. God has delivered us countless times, and we should always be appreciative of His deliverance.

As I look back over my life, I can see the staff of the Shepherd as nothing but grace. In fact, I'm not alone. He has given grace in multiple ways to us all. He also demonstrates the staff as deliverance. He delivers us from the strongholds of life and if He decides not to remove the certain infirmities, He gives us the grace to endure them. We have had many close calls in life, but the deliverance of the Shepherd graces us with His staff and gives us deliverance. He has brought us to safety and rescued us with His shepherding compassion.

The Shepherd has given us such grace that cannot be denied. David is one who certainly knows about the grace of God in his life. Do you value the grace of God in your life? The plethora of things we do not deserve are given by God's grace, and we should be thankful. The staff of the Shepherd gives us grace, and although we don't deserve many things we still experience it. We have personal struggles and setbacks and sins that should expose us, but the grace of God.

David knows how valuable the presence of God is in his life and he solidifies that by saying, "Thou art with me." He changes his language from the third person (the Lord) to the second person (Thou art with me). When we go through dark moments, particularly moments that seems dark as death, you certainly need Him with you. Therefore, when we recognize His presence in good times, it brings a great calm. But when you are in some dangerously dark situations, we need Him to be with us to render security.

The valley moments of darkness and danger will be detrimental if we didn't have the Shepherd. While in the valley, sheep would sometimes fall in the ravines and the Shepherd would rescue them from their current danger. Have you ever had that experience? He saved you, right on time. Yes, even in the ravines, grace is still valid. God's grace will always find you wherever you are. Dr. Jeremiah Wrights (pastor emeritus of the Trinity United Church of Christ in Chicago Illinois) once said, "God will never lead you where grace cannot sustain you." You should know how important the grace of God is in your life, and no matter where you are, grace can locate you. If you are going through moments of difficulty, grace can keep you. If you are going through misery, grace can keep you. Grace keeps us because it's sufficient for us.

The shepherd would not only deliver the sheep in the pasture, no, He also delivers in the valley. The good thing about the valley is, the Shepherd is with the sheep even when it appears to be dark. Therefore, while we go through dark experiences, the presence of the Shepherd gives us hope that it will indeed pass.

The presence of the Shepherd makes a difference because He's certainly necessary. Therefore, when you are going through perilous moments and valley experiences of life know that the help of the Shepherd will allow you to overcome your situational struggles. While you are in the valley, don't give up. Although it's dark and discouraging, don't give up. The Shepherd is with you and He will protect you from this unpleasant experience. Do you trust the Shepherd to be with you? If so, He will be with you to preserve and protect you in the valley.

Don't allow your confidence in your Shepherd to waiver, trust Him. He will never leave you nor forsake you. He will be with you until the end of the world. Have hope in Him and He will deliver you with His staff. Therefore, His divine presence and protection are with you. You can win because He's with you and protects you. Furthermore, keep the faith and trust in God because His deliverance is accessible and available. This is why fear is not necessary because He's with you. You need comfort in the valley and the only way comfort comes is by the presence of the Shepherd, and it's not just any presence because His presence is divine.

Comfort is needful on this Christian journey. It is important to possess because it comes from God and anything that comes from God is essential and relevant. David says that discipline, correction, and deliverance gives him comfort. The psalmist uses an interesting word for comfort, *nāham*. It's a verb meaning "to be sorry, to pity, to comfort, to avenge." David honestly confesses that the rod of God caused him to feel sorry especially when he has been disciplined by God. Also, he understands that the rod is given to protect him from enemies. In addition, He renders His staff as an intricate part of His collection and collaboration of comfort.

He states, "The rod and staff comfort me," which indicates comfort comes from God in multiple and mysterious ways. He gives comfort when you need it the most. God wants to give you the essentials for the journey, and comfort is necessary. The world is filled with trouble and chaos, and this is why comfort is so important. When you look at the news, the evidence is clear, the world is in bad condition. Therefore, when you look around, you see that trouble is on every hand and is ever present. However, you hold on because you understand that your protector will secure you, and that attitude gives you comfort.

When the staff has played a vital part in your life, it gives one the assurance of the deliverance of God. When you go through episode after episode and experience deliverance, you should be encouraged rather than discouraged because God has a way of blessing you even under difficult circumstances. Appreciate your comfort because many persons do not have it. Therefore, if you have it consider yourself blessed. Shepherds desired for their sheep to be comfortable even while in dangerous surroundings. Even in the valley, the Shepherd is there and He desires for you to trust Him despite your discomfort. He wants you to make it and survive, but you must appreciate peace and comfort while going through the valley process.

The world has many problems and it appears that the problems of the world are actually getting worse. However, the child of God must understand that God-given comfort is, in fact, an essential part of our relationship with Him. In this relationship, He wants us to have comfort and know that He's God all by Himself. He also has the passion to give His children comfort while experiencing stressful times. Life is filled with troubling times and treacherous valleys; however, the blessing of knowing the comfort of the Shepherd is near gives the flock security and serenity. Would you feel better if you knew that your protector and provider was with you at all times? David has confidence in God because he understands that whatever situation he experiences his Shepherd is present. We are no different than David. He is with us in our difficult experiences and His desire for us is to have personal peace.

The staff of the Shepherd is to guide the sheep even in the darkest moments of their valley experiences. Life is filled with tipping points and tough moments but the presence of the Shepherd will give comfort in a dark and dangerous environment. Therefore, trust the Shepherd with all of your heart in those dangerous places and dark times of your life, and He will help you to endure. The nature of a shepherd is not only to lead sheep, the shepherd also defends sheep.

Martin Luther says, "This presence of the Lord is not to be perceived with the five senses; faith alone sees it, which is sure of the fact, that the Lord is nearer to us than our own-selves." The blessing of knowing the Shepherd is with you gives absolute comfort. When life constricts you with a strong chokehold and tries to take away from you the very essence of your being, you will need divine help. Yes, divine help is the only thing that can get you through the episodic perils you encounter. David has comfort because his comfort is not in himself, it's in his God.

He, in fact, knows the valley is not an easy experience, but he survives the valley by the leadership of his Shepherd.

The struggles and strains of life are real, and sometimes, it feels as though we are alone in our personal valleys. Therefore, the perils faced in the valley is not the end because the Shepherd gives a package of protection that comforts His sheep with benefits. When you went through that turbulent time but still landed, and the Shepherd kept you when you couldn't actually keep yourself and He does it by His rod and staff.

Although sheep experience darkness and the assumption of death in the valley, something still is working together for good of the flock. The Shepherd is there! Therefore, one fact that cannot be denied is the flock is guided, blessed, and protected, while in the valley and still have no lack. David has confidence in his Shepherd and it's for certain He protects him. David says in Psalm 34:7 (NKJV), "The angel of the LORD encamps all around those who fear Him and delivers them. Never assume that He's not there because He encamps, *ḥānāh*, a verb meaning "to pitch one's tent, encamp." It also refers to pitching a tent in a specific location. The Shepherd has access to the sheep and will go to the full extent of securing them. A true shepherd protects his sheep; they are also concerned about their sheep because they are connected to their sheep because of their relationship.

A true shepherd is concerned about giving the essentials for the sheep. In fact, these words are spoken by Christ as He declares His title as "The Good Shepherd."

> I am the good shepherd. The good shepherd gives His life for the sheep. But a hireling, he who is not the shepherd, one who does not own the sheep, sees the wolf coming and leaves the sheep and flees; and the wolf catches the sheep and scatters them. The hireling flees because he is a hireling and does not care about the sheep. I am the good

shepherd; and I know My sheep, and am known by My own. As the Father knows Me, even so I know the Father; and I lay down My life for the sheep. (Jn 10:11–15, NKJV)

A true shepherd is there for his sheep to support, protect, and give provision for them. When the wolves approach the flock, the shepherd protects them from their enemies to show his love for them. God loves you. He desires for the sheep of His pasture to become closer to Him. We, too, must understand God does the same for us. When we need provision, He gives it. When we need protection, He offers it. That's a true shepherd. He gives awesome shepherding care for His sheep. Therefore, when we face tribulations and difficulties we must know that we can bear the temptation. Paul wrote to the Corinthian church about overcoming adversity. In 1 Corinthians 10:13 (NKJV), "No temptation has overtaken you except such as is common to man; but God is faithful, who will not allow you to be tempted beyond what you are able, but with the temptation will also make the way of escape, that you may be able to bear it."

You are a winner because of the Shepherd; in fact, you are a winner because through Christ we have conquering power. Paul explained to the Romans how we are more than conquerors in Romans 8:37–39 (NKJV), "Yet in all these things we are more than conquerors through Him who loved us. For I am persuaded that neither death nor life, nor angels nor principalities nor powers, nor things present nor things to come, nor height nor depth, nor any other created thing, shall be able to separate us from the love of God which is in Christ Jesus our Lord. You can make it because of the conquering nature Christ gives us. Although we have many difficult circumstances coming from different directions, we must be encouraged because we were made to conquer the situations of life because of "The Good Shepherd."

71

Divine Preparation

David's Shepherd is a God of order. He's in order and not out of order. Sometimes, we experience things in the natural that work, and all of a sudden, they are "out of order." God is a divine preparer; His divine preparation may seem out of order to humanity, but supernaturally, it is in order. The ways of God are so mysterious to man that sometimes we may actually feel that God is out of order simply because He doesn't work according to our timetable.

David has an extraordinary encounter. He experiences the supernatural sovereignty of his Shepherd. In this experience, he sees the power of God displayed to him in an unusual way. He's blessed with the favor of God from a perspective of preparation and order. Therefore, while in this place of preparation, he sees the order of God in a very meticulous way. David experiences the favor of God on a table. However, on this table, he doesn't prepare the table personally, his Shepherd does.

David honestly confesses his Shepherd is a provider, protector, and preparer. He sees the order of his Shepherd after the Shepherd distributed discipline and directional provision for him. God is in order and never dysfunctional. At the table, David changes his linguistic tone from a shepherding perspective to a hosting perspective. David uses a riveting word to prepare, the word 'ārak, a verb meaning "to arrange, to set in order, to prepare." David sees the order of the Shepherd out of all places, in the valley at a table. His journey has transitioned from green pastures, still waters, paths of righteousness, the valley of the shadow of death, and now, a table (in the valley).

While David is at the table, he may be very well wondering why God has put him at a place of such precision, order, and significance. It's apparent he's at this place because the Shepherd led him there. God has treasures of goodness for those sheep who allow Him to lead them. In Psalm 31, David testifies of the treasures of God's goodness. Psalm 31:19 (NKJV), "Oh, how great is Your goodness, Which You have laid up for those who fear You, Which You have prepared for those who trust in You In the presence of the sons of men!" In this Psalm, David acknowledges the blessings of God come to those who fear Him and trust Him. In order for a shepherd to lead, sheep must trust their lead.

The table is awaiting David because he has allowed his Shepherd to lead him and not him trying to reverse roles and lead the Shepherd. Therefore, the Shepherd places David at this table and proceeds to host him, and might I say, host him with excellence. David used the word šulḥān for "table" which is indicative of hosting a guest to fulfill their needs and supply provision. The table is also a symbol of the favor of God and should not be taken for granted because anyone can sit at the table. David experiences the favor of God at this table because he's the visitor and God is the host. This imagery is also a portrait of the relationship between the sheep and Shepherd—they have fellowship and a bond. However, there's something interesting about this scenery; this awesome hosting experience is still in the valley.

In hilly terrains, flat surfaces were called "tables," and the shepherd would allow them to eat there after a difficult day of labor. The shepherd would provide a feast for them at the table, and then allow them to rest because sheep would eat then sleep. In addition, the shepherd would give them grace and mercy at the table. Therefore, God gives His people grace and mercy as well. You know we don't deserve every blessing God gives us, but often He sits us down at a table and lavishly provides us providential provision. Furthermore, this is why it's so important for us to remain humble because someone else could be sitting in our place. Actually, as David has changed his vernacular from the perspective of shepherding into hosting; however, the principle is still the same. In like manner, as the Shepherd provided for him in the green pastures, He now does it at the table.

We must acknowledge and be aware that the provision of God is not limited to a certain space or place. The Shepherd teaches a lesson we should apply to our faith, and that is providential provision and protection will work in different places. David transitions and testifies the Shepherd sets the feast on the table before him. He uses the word *pāneh*, which means "in the face." At this richly provisional table, the Shepherd places the blessings of the feast right in David's face. Have you ever had blessings like that before? Some blessings were right in your face. Contrastingly, some have the blessings of the Shepherd in their face and sometimes they are not appreciative of them, nor do they ever acknowledge them as well.

Sometimes, we have the blessings of the Shepherd in our lives and we easily can take them for granted. However, some do not take the blessings of God for granted because they are aware that those blessings can very well be in someone else's possession. Are you thankful like David? Are you grateful and thankful for the hosting presence of God? He sets us in hosting capacities that places us on other levels. In fact, the levels are so vibrant and beautiful that enemies see the blessings. In the east, shepherds would be with their sheep even while their predators surround them. The meaning I believe David is trying to get us to see is the blessings of God don't cease because your predators have you surrounded. No, they continue. The Shepherd protects and provides for the sheep even while the enemies of the sheep are present.

Have you ever been blessed in the surrounding of your enemies and the only thing they could do was spectate? When you have a practical relationship with the Shepherd, He will give you what you need, not only in pastures that are green but also at the table which is surrounded by enemies and out of all places, the valley. You know you have the favor of God when your predators can't have your blessings nor take them, but they can see them distributed from the Shepherd into your possession. Therefore, sheep feel safe and secure when they recognize the Shepherd's care, especially when their enemies cannot interfere with them.

Sheep have an authentic sense of security and not an artificial one, especially when they know they can depend on their shepherd. For the most part, we, too, are the same. We have comfort and confidence when we have an encounter with the divine. The presence of enemies is no threat to the sheep because of the presence of the Shepherd.

In addition, the sheep experience another factor of the Shepherd's hosting and that is His anointing. Davis somehow realizes how important the anointing is in his life. The psalmist honestly confesses, the Shepherd anoints his head with oil. To anoint—*dāšēn*—a verb meaning "to be fat, to grow fat, to fatten," or in a figurative sense, "to anoint, to satisfy." However, the diversity this word gives carries such a statement about the anointing of our God. David recognizes how important the anointing is in his life. He's aware of the fact, he can't grow, he can't be fattening spiritually, and he can't be satisfied without the anointing of his Shepherd.

In the east, shepherds would anoint sheep's heads with oil because of certain facts. In ancient times, the anointing would take place before festival meals and the aroma had a very sweet smell. Additionally, while the guest was in the hosting seat, it was customary the Shepherd anoint them. The psalmist declares this process of anointing did not start out of order, it begins at the head. The eastern shepherds would anoint the heads of sheep because of "parasites." Insects would often get in the ears and nasal cavities and lay eggs and a larva would form and agitate the sheep.

The agitation would be so discomforting to the sheep it would bang its head on something and try to stop the constant agitation. Therefore, the shepherd would anoint the sheep's head with oil and that would cause the insects to slide and that would be difficult for the insects to lay eggs. The anointing is designed and present to rid you of agitating and irritating parasites. Just as sheep have parasites in the natural, we, too, have them in the natural and also the spiritual. Yes, you have irritants in your life and the only remedy for your irritants is the anointing. In the valley, the Shepherd hosts David with a spirit of excellence and prepares divinely for him. In addition, He also provided the anointing in the valley.

The IVP Bible Background Old Testament Commentary says, "Banqueters in the ancient world were often treated by a generous host to fine oils that would be used to anoint their foreheads. This provided not only a glistening sheen to their countenance but also would have added a fragrance to their persons and the room." My friend, you can make it with God's anointing. The anointing is needed to be victorious over the enemy. We need the anointing to defeat the enemy and his soldiers. One of the problems the church has made was selecting persons to serve in ministry while they have no anointing to serve. When God has anointed you, you trust and depend on Him to lead and guide you to your destiny. When you possess the anointing, you are blessed indeed. You have what others desire to possess but do not have because they are strangers unto salvation. The anointing is prevalent in your life when you allow the Holy Spirit to indwell you with His anointing. In fact, the very thing that gets you through the valley is because you are anointed.

When you are anointed, you are blessed. When eastern shepherds anointed sheep, they placed a blessing on them. Would it be great to be blessed by the Shepherd? The anointing is nothing but the Shepherd's blessing in your life. In fact, the reason why the enemy is limited harming you because you are anointed by the Shepherd. Although you are anointed by the Shepherd, this doesn't mean you are exempt from the difficulties of life. Therefore, while going through the adverse moments of the valley, the Shepherd gives you divine preparation, coupled with the anointing.

David experiences the hosting excellence of God while encountering divine preparation. He has an encounter with *Jehovah–Saboath* (the Lord of Hosts) where God hosts His guest. The passage 1 Samuel 1:3 (NKJV) states, "This man went up from his city yearly to worship and sacrifice to the LORD of hosts in Shiloh. Also the two sons of Eli, Hophni and Phinehas, the priests of the LORD, were there." When you experience the hosting excellence of God, you encounter His presence in a different way. He actually shows you that He knows how to serve you even in the adverse circumstances of the valley. The Shepherd knows how to treat His sheep and takes care of them despite what they go through and where they experience difficulty. God will take care of you in the pleasures of life and also the pains of life as well.

Never overlook the hosting capacity of God. He hosts us with His grace and mercy and through a "spirit of excellence." The anointing of God demonstrates the power of God in the manner of blessing toward His flock. David confesses the Shepherd "anoints his head with oil and his cup runs over" indicates the sheep are blessed by the Shepherd. When you are blessed, you are anointed. The anointing God gives is soothing. The imagery of David's testimony displays a frequent blessing the Shepherd gives to the sheep. This specific blessing takes place in the valley. Yes, the Shepherd blesses the sheep in the valley. Isn't it good to know that God will bless you wherever you are? You are anointed by God from head to toe and His blessings are not stagnant, they flow.

God has a continuous blessing for you, just allow Him to lead you not only to green pastures, still waters, but He also leads in the dark and cold valley. Therefore, what should you do while in the valley? Continue to trust Him. In like manner, if He led you to the green pasture, He will lead you in the valley. In essence, the blessing of the Shepherd is in the valley, just like it is in the green pastures. However, the intriguing thing about the valley is the anointing actually is recognized by David in the valley rather than the green pastures. I certainly believe the anointing is best shown when we go through adversity in the valleys of life. Often, persons think of the anointing in the sunny days, but many misunderstand that the anointing is there also in the dark valleys.

The Pulpit Commentary says, "Life not only involves work but also conflict. Our enemies are numerous, powerful, and cruel. The fight is fierce, prolonged, and exhausting. Yet, spread by invisible hands is the table in the wilderness, in the presence of our grim-visaged enemies who, while looking on, are restrained by some irresistible spell from harming." Although we may not see the Shepherd, He and His anointing are there. The divine preparer gives us protection, provision, and preparation in the valley.

Divine Prosperity

I'm sure you have had some valley experiences and due to the difficulties of defeat, you may have assumed The Shepherd is not with you, He's with you and He has meticulously prepared your journey divinely. God makes a way for us in many ways, therefore He desires for us to understand His intentions are the best for us because He's a God of order and arrangement and not a God of disorder and disorganization. My friend, you are so blessed because the Shepherd has given you a "my cup runs over" experience. When your cup runs over, what actually happens? Your cup runs over because He has anointed you with blessing and anointing. Therefore, you do not have to worry about the struggles of life because your Shepherd will take care of you. Furthermore, when you have this type of experience, you realize that you actually have more than a double portion—you have an overflow.

What do you have when you have a "my cup runs over" experience? You have God's special favor and the "fat" of God. David mentions, "My cup runs over." The interesting thing to notice about the cup is the meaning of the word. David uses the Hebrew word *kôs* which means a small cup or goblet. These were small drinking cups and goblets. However, we do know that the anointing is not small, it's sacred.

Have you noticed something significant about your cup? Your cup is significantly special if you've paid attention to it. Can I tell you about your cup? Firstly, your cup is a vessel that's empty; secondly, although, your cup is empty, it needs to be filled; thirdly, your cup needs to be filled with not just anything; finally, your cup needs to be filled with the anointing . . . and not only filled, it actually runs over. What does David mean by his cup runs over? David uses *rewāyāh* which simply means "abundance." In addition, the figurative meaning of the word means "the cup of life and blessing from the Lord." Aren't you thankful you have life, blessing, and abundance? You should be. The very fact you are alive should cause you to be thankful, also, when blessing and abundance is being experienced by you from the Shepherd should cause you even more joy!

Therefore, it is imperative that we understand the Shepherding factor in our lives. It is the Shepherd who anoints, then fills, and then allow overflowing. Haddon W. Robinson says in his book *Trusting the Shepherd*:

> To draw the water, a shepherd used a leather bucket at the end of a long rope. The bucket held about three quarts, and the shepherd had to let it down and draw it up hand-over-hand. Then he poured the water into large stone cups beside the well. It was a long and tiring process. If a shepherd had fifty sheep, he might have to draw water for two hours or more to allow the sheep to drink all they wanted.

The implication is a true shepherd will go to the fullest length to make for certain the flock needs are met. With the overflowing of the Shepherd appears in your life, just know that you are an anointed individual with an overflow. In fact, when we have this type of experience, it is because God gives more than enough. The anointing you have is special. In addition, what makes it even more special is when you have an overflow of it. Actually, when the overflowing takes place, it actually runs over. Now, when it runs over, the Shepherd lets you know how abundantly blessed and anointed you are. When you are anointed, you are highly favored by God to do special things in life. The special things you do is simply because God has favored you for such a time as this to experience the overflow.

Another additional meaning of the overflow gives an intoxicating effect when the pouring takes place in the cup. The ancient text suggests and uses the language as being "filled to the brim." This expression is taken from ancient belief. The belief is the cup drinker is the guest and the owner of the cup is the host. The host gives the cup to the guest and fills it beyond capacity because an overflow is necessary and nothing is too good for the guest. Doesn't that sound like God? He gives and gifts us with not normal capacity but overflowing capacity.

In fact, this act of generosity implies the Shepherd does not have to give the sheep anything, this is done by grace. God's favor is the key to understanding it's His generosity. You do not get the overflow on your own, God gives it. He gives it as grace. Therefore, we should not take for granted the importance of the impartation of God's grace. For the simple reason that we are no better than anyone else; we fall sometimes, we make pivotal mistakes; but He still graces us with His generosity.

A vital lesson about the cup is the drinking does not begin at the bottom or middle, it starts at the brim. Therefore, since it begins at the brim of the cup indicates it starts at the beginning and not the end. With that being said, when we are filled, we are anointed. Our anointing doesn't come from beneath, it comes from above. Furthermore, when He anoints us, He fills us. We can never get enough of the anointing. The anointing is what we need to fulfill our journey. The Shepherd anoints us to the degree of realizing enemies and foes are no longer relevant. Yes, at the hosting table, the Shepherd gives His sheep what's needed for their journey and that's His anointing that certainly runs over.

When we recognize the blessings God gives us comes from God, we must understand God is the ultimate source that blesses us. It's not ourselves it's God. Therefore, we should be humble and thankful of God's sovereignty because He is the only source who sovereignly blesses up. Some individuals are very successful and many have achieved many things to cause them to live an abundant lifestyle. However, one thing many fail to realize is understanding who supplies such a lifestyle for them. I know you perhaps have a good career due to your sacrifices of the past by getting your degree in a certain field of interest you've pursued. In addition, some have gained much not by gaining a degree, some just know how to hustle and make a good living for themselves and provide exceptionally well for their families. Although, the degree is earned, some hustle successfully, but they may not be aware of the specifics of how they are blessed and who blesses them. Actually, some have a conceited scope of their success and fail to understand God is the ultimate source that distributes their blessings to them. There are many who make good salaries, have good pensions, and retirements, but who gives it? God. God, the true Shepherd gives us the blessings we need in order for us to enjoy them (1 Tim. 6:17).

I know you are successful, but where did your success originate from? I know you have made major accomplishments, but who gave you the grace to attain them? I know you have a lucrative salary from your vocation, but who gave you the opportunity to make that lucrative compensation? I know you live in the home of your dreams, but who allowed you to actually live in your dream home? I know the vehicle you drive is an eye-catcher, but who allows you to drive what you drive? Simply God!

David mentions a combination of things that actually happen at the banquet feast. The Shepherd anoints the head and his cup runs over. Such benefits like this come from God and Him alone. Therefore, when God gives His blessings to us, we should acknowledge Him and thank Him for His benevolent generosity. Unfortunately, some persons do not offer God any thanks because of their personal pride.

Failure to revere God with honor because of the reality of pride is dangerous. In fact, scripture reminds us of the danger of a prideful person. The proverbial writer states in Proverbs 16:18 (NKJV), "Pride goes before destruction, And a haughty spirit before a fall."

Secondly, in Proverbs 11:2 (NKJV), "When pride comes, then comes shame; But with the humble is wisdom."

Thirdly, in Proverbs 8:13 (NKJV), "The fear of the LORD is to hate evil; Pride and arrogance and the evil way And the perverse mouth I hate." Fourthly, Proverbs 29:23 (NKJV), "A man's pride will bring him low, But the humble in spirit will retain honor." Solomon I believe wants us to know how important it is to have humility rather than pride. Many individuals claim responsibility for their own accomplishments, however, failing to realize God is truly deserving of honor is disrespectful to His deity.

God's way of shepherding gives the best blueprint or example for human leaders to lead. Unfortunately, all do not follow the mandate of Christ, let alone God's design for relational leadership. Therefore, we must understand with clarity the imperativeness of God's abundance in our lives. He's definitely the God of more than enough. He gives us what we need and even more. We worship a more-than-enough God. He supplies us with what we need; so, therefore, we can rest in His abiding abundance continually with confidence.

With that being said, for we know that what we have comes from God and Him alone. More often than not, humanity tries to take the credit for God by arrogantly assuming they've made it this far by themselves. However, the reality is, we will not be who and what we are if it had not been for God's grace functioning in our lives daily. This is why we should never get beside ourselves because we are limited, but God is unlimited. There is a consistent trend of arrogance by some who are firmly convinced they are their source. However, we who believe know we are not the source, but God definitely is, and we give Him all the glory. When you are abundantly blessed no one has to remind you. You know it for yourself. However, some are aware of the blessings God gives them, but often, they lose memory of who has blessed them. Therefore, we must remain humble and continue to reverence God for His sovereignty and abundance of His blessings. You know undoubtingly that God has blessed you tremendously, and you know that the power is not of yourself, it's from God. However, in order to know God, you must know who you are as well and realize God gives His abundant blessings to His children.

We must be consistently reminded of the way shepherds protect their sheep and give them provision, so does our Heavenly Father. He puts us in places we never thought we would be. He blesses us with things we thought we'd never have, and He gives us a spiritual bond with relationship and fellowship. Actually, this is why we should be thankful for the anointing and overflowing God gives.

Have you ever had some overflow encounters that gave you the conclusion of knowing God was the cause of your overflow? There are many scriptural accounts of the abundance of God when He gave more than enough through His Son. If you recall, there's a narrative about Jesus feeding a great multitude with much. However, through the lens of humanity, it may seem small; nevertheless, it concluded with an abundant miracle. The narrative states there were two resources essential for this miracle to take place: bread and fish.

With these resources, an abundant miracle took place with what some would consider being so little, but in Jesus's hands is considered to be much. Jesus took two tiny fish (sardines) and five barley loaves of bread and fed a multitude of five thousand men and remaining women and children. In addition, after they were fed, they didn't leave empty handed. They had enough for leftovers. This is what I call overflow.

An additional Biblical account is recorded in Luke's gospel where Peter has fished all night, and due to his efforts, he has not caught anything. No doubt he's fatigued and has decided to call it a night by washing their nets. After resigning for the day, Jesus advises him to launch out into the deep. Actually, Peter didn't really want to launch out because he said, "Nevertheless at Your word I will let it down. As a result of him letting it down, he caught a great number of fish to the degree that their nets were breaking, to add the boat began to sink, sounds familiar? Overflow.

Another scriptural account is documented in John's gospel where Jesus, Mary, and His disciples were invited to a wedding feast in Cana of Galilee. After hearing the news about the absence of wine, Mary advises Jesus to perform a miracle at the wedding. He responds to her and says, "His time is not yet," nevertheless, Mary insisted to the servants to do whatever He commands of them. Jesus instructs them to fill each water pot (six of them) with water, and they filled it to the brim, and after the master sampled the wine, he suggested the wine Jesus gave was the absolute best. The emphasis of these stories is indicative of the Shepherd and sheep relationship. The Shepherd will not only anoint, but He will also give overflowing experiences. I'd like to also label this as not only abundance but superabundance! Yes, God superabundantly blesses us with our needs and desires because the Shepherd cares for *His* sheep.

Every situation we face God knows how to superabundantly supply provision. When you need Him, He's available. Now, when you are in need of joy, He gives it; when peace is absent,

He gives it; when resources are drained, He provides; when sick, He's a physician. There is no reason to become overwhelmed with problems and difficulties because His supersized abundance is always accessible to us because He desires intimate fellowship with His flock.

Part Three

He Guarantees Us

Surely goodness and mercy shall follow me all the days of my life and I will dwell in the house of the LORD Forever.

—Psalm 23:6

The last and final provisional need God meets for His sheep is their eternal needs. This psalm transitions into eternity. David makes a firm suggestion about his life and eternality when he uses the word *surely*. The word *surely* implies only and surely which indicates there's no doubt in his confidence about his life and his future. David has tremendous confidence in his life, it is proven in his present state, also in his future, because God is a part of it.

Do you have confidence? If not, you cannot survive the valleys of life; however, if so, you can become victorious in life and also be excited about your future. Often, many persons do not go to the next level or dimension of their lives because they have an absence of confidence. However, those who are confident seem to have the best things in life and that's simply because they have a "surely" attitude. It's amazing how persons achieve much when they have a surely attitude about their relationship with

God, their life, dreams, and future. When they possess this type of attitude, they will never be defeated, they will always progress.

David's confidence level of having his eternal needs met is certainly high because he has no doubt about his future with God. Again, the Hebrew word surely *'ak* means "only" or "surely," therefore, David is sure that certain things will be in fellowship in his life because he seems to possess an optimal level of confidence. David apparently had no doubt because he utters *surely*; he has extreme confidence in his future state with God and seems to be excited about his new journey.

Divine Pleasure

David seems to have a prophetic voice in his level of confidence because he realizes how important goodness and mercy is to him, not only in his present life, but his life to come. This confident level has something to do with his attitude and how he sees himself in his Lord's house. Do you ever see yourself in a better place in the future? David surely does! In like manner, we should see our future better than our present. Therefore, when we understand the essentials of our lives, we glean to understand our purpose is clearly in God's hands.

Why is purpose so important? David declares goodness and mercy shall follow him all the days of his life. Actually, that sounds like purpose to me. David clarifies his purpose when he utters that goodness *ṭôḇ* which means, "good, well-pleasing, fruitful, morally correct, proper, and convenient." I must say, that's a good life to live when things are good, well-pleasing, fruitful, morally correct, and things are convenient. David says he will experience these awesome experiences on "earth," and he doesn't have to wait until the sweet by and by. Life is good and we should expect the best while we experience it on this side of eternity. We should encounter good moments on earth yet while we live; there will, in fact, be moments that will be well-pleasing (every day is not a bad experience), and when we encounter those moments, they will result as being fruitful. In addition, what makes things even more rewarding when we are morally correct and when we are committed to that is definitely proper and convenient. The good life is experienced because the Shepherd will never leave us nor forsake us. The goodness of God is not only constituted for a local area, it covers the world. The psalmist suggests in Psalm 33:4–5 (NKJV), "For the word of the LORD is right, And all His work is done in truth. He loves righteousness and justice; the earth is full of the goodness of the LORD. All of the earth experiences the goodness of God, and He saturates it with His goodness. In fact, we can't hide from the goodness of God because His goodness is omnipresent.

The implication of understanding the goodness of God is knowing we will encounter His goodness while we live. For we actually know that God is good to all, although some never appreciate it and some do. Actually, when we experience His goodness, we come to gain knowledge about His nature regarding His goodness. Therefore, when we are educated more about His nature, we understand the agricultural relational example of the relationship between the shepherd and sheep.

Sheep have good, well-pleasing, and fruitful moments in the presence of the shepherd. Just as earthly sheep have such comfort, then the spiritual sheep know their shepherd is good. In like manner, we should be thankful for our Shepherd. He's so good to us; He blesses us beyond measure and gives the provisions and protection we need in order to survive the tough moments of life. The goodness of God is essential in our lives and it satisfies, secures, and saturates us to the brim of the cup. God surely knows how to give us well pleasing moments on earth.

All of David's days are not bad because he now looks at his circumstances in a good way because he understands his Shepherd is a part of his future. When you and I have the presence of God with us, it should give us joy and peace. We should have joy and peace not only for the present but for the future as well. When you are in the presence of God, joy and peace births confidence in God, then you can rely on Him with no worries and experience His divine peace.

Divine Pardon

The good life is when you have God and possess a relationship with Him and recognize Him as your source, supplier, sustainer, and savior. Therefore, as we venture through life, we must understand God will supply our needs and give us the desire of our hearts and take us to the next levels of our lives if we delight in Him. God is good, and yes, He's good all the time. He allows His goodness to follow us. In addition, not only does David thank God for goodness, but he also realizes how much he needs the mercy of God in his life. David recognizes the importance of the mercy God gives. He uses the Hebrew word *ḥeseḏ*, indicating "kindness, loving-kindness, mercy, goodness, faithfulness, love, acts of kindness." The interesting indication about the word *mercy* displays to us about the benevolent and compassionate mercy of God. The additional usage of the word *hesed* also shows God's total commitment to you in the Shepherd/sheep relationship.

God has unconditional love for His children just as a parent loves their children. Of course, parents should have unconditional love for their child. Your child is not perfect, but he or she is still your child. Your son may be a felon and your daughter a drug addict, but they're still your children. Although you may not like what your child does, you still love him or her for who they are—your child. In fact, you might not even like your child at times, but that's your child. In like manner, God does not like what we do at times but He's still our Father. David not only realizes the goodness of God in his past, present, and future. He understands he experiences the goodness of God because His mercy is unconditional.

Experiencing God's mercy is paramount to our existence because we are nothing without it. Honestly, when we are given mercy, something has been extended to us that we don't deserve. We do not deserve God's grace, but He gives it to us in spite of. Therefore, we should be appreciative for His acts of kindness that are distributed to us. We have been given mercy perpetually, and sometimes, it's not appreciated by some who do not value its importance. For we know we have sinned and fallen short many times, but He gives us perpetual grace and mercy. In fact, the psalmist declares God has not dealt with us according to the sins we have committed (Psalm 103).

God has been so good to us. Actually, if you've taken a certified account of the grace God has given, you would be thankful for His grace, compassion, benevolence, goodness, and faithfulness. The greatest act of kindness God demonstrated was the death of Christ on the cross on Calvary. Grace and mercy should never be taken for granted because it's God's way of showing His compassionate heart toward humanity. No one should ever look down on anyone because we are all recipients of God's wonderful grace and mercy. While meditating on the grace of our God, something I noticed about God's grace that totally blessed my life, that is, the grace of God gives us opportunities to survive after failure, correct our wrongs, and be sovereignly sustained by His grace.

God promises His mercy and we can depend upon His promise. Since we have a promise-keeping God, we can certainly trust in His promise of abundant mercy. The psalmist declares in Psalm 89:28 (NKJV), "My mercy I will keep for him forever, And My covenant shall stand firm with him." As I stated prior, we should be thankful for mercy and be appreciative that He has not dealt with us according to our sin. Therefore, God's abundant mercy should be valued and appreciated because it is divinely promised. Just the thought of eternal mercy shows the compassionate side of our Shepherd. He promises His compassion and without it, we wouldn't last.

We have been wrong in a lot of things. I know I have. I remember very vividly my sister and I did chores at home, and I mean we worked hard. My parents gave us a weekly allowance and they rewarded us according to what they thought was fair. Honestly, I mean my sister and I toiled (really worked hard) that week, and we were really expecting a great reward the next week. However, we were unaware that our parents had made plans just as we've done. We were expecting an increase that week because we worked hard the week prior. Interestingly enough, they planned to joke with us and I remember my father handing my sister and me two dollars each, and the expression on our faces showed extreme disappointment. Actually, their original plans were to give us twenty-five dollars instead of two (us not knowing), but when they gave it to us, we told them to keep it and they did just that. Then my father and mother told us that we were going to initially receive twenty-five dollars each, but because we were disrespectful of their prank, they decided to keep it all.

The vital lesson is, although we reacted wrongly to our parents and they gave us absolutely nothing, the blessing is, we still were under their roof, food was on the table, clothing on our backs, shoes were on our feet, and they still claimed us as their children. In like manner, God gives us abundant grace and mercy. Although we deserve worse, He still graces us with unconditional love.

We have done things God didn't like, but He's still our Heavenly Father. Although He may not approve of our faults and failures, He still gives His grace and mercy to show us His compassionate heart. Certainly, we have not been good all the time, but He extends grace and mercy toward us, although in reality, we deserve much worse. To add, this is why we should value God's unconditional love, because He loves us despite the condition.

Divine Persistence

David states goodness and mercy follows him all the days of his life. There are some things we rather not follow us, such as our past, shortcomings, failures, and etc. However, the good news about David's confidence is that he's not focused on his failures and shortcomings; he only dwells on the combination of goodness and mercy following him while he lives. The Preacher's Homiletic Commentary says that goodness and mercy, "shall follow me all the days of my life. Through all its changes, its shade and sunshine, its perils and deliverances, its sorrows and joys, to its close." The reality is, whatever state you are in, goodness and mercy follow you consistently.

Often, people dwell on the negative circumstances of life and very rarely on the positive. David does not have this disposition; with all the sinful acts David committed, he chooses not to focus on the negative; he focuses on the positive because he has confidence in his Shepherd. He firmly focuses on the goodness and mercy of God. This is the common denominator that proves David walks through his valley encounters. When you have a relationship with the Shepherd you will always have a revelation of the Shepherd that's progressive and not passive.

It takes progressive revelation to focus on your destiny when you know you have done things to perhaps compromise it. The progressive revelation allows us to understand we have a perfect combo—goodness, and mercy. In fact, the perfect combination has you where you are right now in life. Furthermore, in spite of your circumstances, goodness and mercy follows you all the days of your existence. These blissful attributes bless us in specific ways. His goodness supplies our needs and His mercy blot out our sins.

God gives abundantly to us His goodness and mercy and it travels with us wherever we go. The persistence of God's goodness and mercy goes all the way. God's blessings follow us despite our geographical location. You can never get to the pinnacle of your life without persistence. Many experience life being unfulfilled due to the fact they are not persistent enough. Actually, many blessings are forfeited because of the absence of persistence. We often quit when disappointment comes our way and accept whatever life gives us. However, the goodness and mercy of God is diligently persistent; it always follows us.

David did something all of us should do and do it often. David looked back over his life and gave God thanks for giving him goodness and mercy. I look back over my life very often and render thanks to God because of the reality of His goodness and mercy which follows me. In fact, there are things I know I don't deserve, but He gives it because He's a good God and gives grace to all. Although we fall, sin, and make mistakes, He still allows His benevolence to be a part of our lives. We have security in God because He supplies us with such great attributes.

I remember growing up, my sister and I had two loving and providing parents (still do). They provided for us from the rocking of our cradles until it was time for us to respond to life's responsibilities. They were persistent in giving us essential resources, food, shelter, and protection persistently. My parents weren't rich, but they provided for us the best way they could and did it with excellence! In reference to God, our Heavenly Father is rich and has it all, and He provides for us persistently and He gives us the very best, not because we deserved it, but because He has a love that's unconditional.

Divine Palace

David's relationship with God is indeed firm. He testifies about God and their bond. However, there's something interesting about this psalm; David begins the psalm with the Lord. Now, he concludes this psalm with the Lord's house. In fact, David has an earnest desire for the house of the Lord. David knows when a person is no longer living on this side of eternity, they are somewhere else, heaven or hell. Actually, David has extreme confidence in knowing that He will be in the presence of God forever. The confidence this sheep realizes about his Shepherd is knowing he will dwell in the house of the Lord forever.

David switches from all other needs and now focuses on his eternal needs. He definitely knows that he needs to be with God forever. I believe David is talking about heaven. Although, some disagree. David says with firm confidence, "I will dwell." The Hebrew word he uses is *yāšab*, which means "to sit, to dwell, to inhabit, to endure, to stay." The question is, stay where? The house of the Lord. The Hebrew word *bayit* stands for "house," which means a dwelling place or palace. The term *house* does not refer to the temple because kings did not live in the temple (some disagree). David essentially understands that he will be with God in a dwelling place and that dwelling place is not temporal but eternal.

Heaven, that place where we often dwell on, that place where we teach and preach about, is the place David is referring to. Jesus talked about heaven and teaches us lessons on the Father's house in John's gospel.

> Let not your heart be troubled; you believe in God, believe also in Me. In My Father's house are many mansions; if it were not so, I would have told you. I go to prepare a place for you. And if I go and prepare a place for you, I will come again and receive you to Myself; that where I am, there you may be also. And where I go you know, and the way you know." Thomas said to Him, "Lord, we do not know where You are going, and how can we know the way?" Jesus said to him, "I am the way, the truth, and the life. No one comes to the Father except through Me." (Jn 14:1–6, NKJV)

There are many things we will understand when we get to heaven that we don't fully comprehend now. We will look back over our lives and fully understand how the goodness and mercy of God persistently followed us. W. A. VanGemeren says, "The 'experience' with God takes on a transcendental significance, as it gives the believer a taste of everlasting fellowship with God." When we leave this world, we are destined for our new home, in the presence of God. You and I will be in heaven when we leave this planet, and we will be with God forever. Paul assures us in his letter to the Corinthians about the location of those souls who have left the body. "We are confident, yes, well pleased rather to be absent from the body and to be present with the Lord" (2 Cor. 5:8, NKJV)

The word absent is very interesting. Paul uses the word *ekdēméō*; which means away from home, which is from *ek*, from or out of, and *démos*, "people." To go abroad, to part as the parting from the body, the earthly abode of the spirit (2 Cor. 5:6, 8, 9) or to be away or absent from the body and present with the Lord. In addition, the word *present* also has an interesting meaning, *endēméō*; one who is at home, in his own country, or among his own people, which is from en, in, and démos, an organized body of people. To be at home, to be present in any place, or with any person (2 Cor. 5:6, 8–9 [cf. Phil. 1:23]). What Paul is saying when you are in an earthly demographic, you are not at home with God. Therefore, he further explains when you are in heaven, you are at home with God. Wouldn't you be better off if you were in God's eternal presence forever?

Abiding in heaven for eternity will be worth it all! You can look back over your life and see how your Shepherd put you in green pastures and lead you beside still waters. Rejoicing over the testimony of how you made it over into the house of the Lord forever. You and I will make it because of the relationship we have with God. Honestly, you must have a relationship with God to live with Him forever. Without a relationship with God, there's no spiritual connection nor will they be with God for eternity. Therefore, when there is a relationship with the Shepherd, there's spiritual purpose, power, and presence with Him for eternity.

We are looking for that day when we will be with God forever. In fact, sometimes, we often think about it. Yes, we think about that day when we get to heaven and worship God for eternity. When believers leave this world, they will be in the presence of God forever. Often, we have heaven in view. Heaven is our goal and our home for those who have made Christ Lord and Savior. When death comes for the believer, they are absent from their earthly tabernacle and present in their mansion.

The follower of Christ will go to heaven. Yes, we can see heaven in our view. Although we might not be there yet, we know that's our home. We know that prior to getting there, there will be moments of discouragement and despondency en route to heaven. However, we must continue to trust God. When we trust God, we know there's a place better there than here. We will dwell in the house of the Lord forever. It's like a runner in a race, they train and make necessary preparations for their prestigious moment. Although, there's much rehearsing for that one moment of the race. Spending countless hours, days, and perhaps months in training, all for that special moment of attaining the prize. However, it takes much dedication and commitment to achieve the prize.

All of us like prizes and when we get to the judgment seat of Christ, we will receive our prizes in heaven. Paul explains to the Corinthian church about the judgment seat of Christ and what the rewards will be like in heaven. The believers will receive their prize in the bema judgment seat of Christ. This judgment shall come when the church is taken to heaven or raptured, then this judgment shall take place. In this particular judgment, believers (Christians) will be judged and evaluated based upon their faithfulness to Christ, and they will also be rewarded for their quality of life.

> For we must all appear before the judgment seat
> of Christ, that each one may receive the things
> done in the body, according to what he has done,
> whether good or bad. (2 Cor. 5:10, NKJV)

Paul confirms persuasively that all believers will be judged, but our judgment will be different from the unbeliever's judgment. We will appear at the judgment seat of Christ. In this judgment, believers will receive the things they have done in the body, whether good or bad. However, the emphasis is that believers will be in heaven because this verse shows that salvation is not the problem because His children will be in heaven and every one who will be in heaven will be saved.

This saying by Paul is a metaphor "judgment seat" metaphorically means the place where the Lord will sit and evaluate believers for the sole purpose of giving them eternal rewards. *Béma* is even used metaphorically in reference to Christ (Rom. 14:10; 2 Cor. 5:10) in which cases the word has eschatological meaning. We must, therefore, consider these two terms as interchangeable. Both refer to the judgment after death found in Heb. 9:27, "It is appointed unto men once to die, but after this the judgment."

The word *béma* also was an elevated platform where victorious athletes would stand after being victorious to receive their prize. The Corinthians had no problem understanding this metaphor because they had platforms for athletic rewards. Therefore, when believers stand, they will have a reward(s) from Christ. However, some have issues with the words Paul wrote the things done in the body. What Paul is referring to is the actions done in the body during the believer's time of earthly ministry.

In fact, this does not refer nor includes sin because of the judgment that took place on the cross for the sins of humanity. John Macarthur says, "Paul was referring to all those activities believers do during their lifetimes, which relate to their eternal reward and praise from God." The word *done, prásso* of a course of action or conduct, especially of right, duty, virtue, to do, meaning "to exercise and practice." Also, the term *whether good or bad* does not refer to a moral good or evil; however, it refers to comparing worthwhile virtues instead of useless ones. The believer has been forgiven for sins because of Christ's substitutionary sacrifice on the cross for the sins of the world.

In the bema judgment, only believers will be judged. Paul made that clear because he refers to those who have built on the foundation, Jesus Christ (1 Cor. 3:11–12).

> Who then is Paul, and who is Apollos, but ministers through whom you believed, as the Lord gave to each one? I planted, Apollos watered, but God gave the increase. So then neither he who plants is anything, nor he who waters, but God who gives the increase. Now he who plants and he who waters are one, and each one will receive his own reward according to his own labor. For we are God's fellow workers; you are God's field, you are God's building. According to the grace of God which was given to me, as a wise master builder I have laid the foundation, and another builds on it. But let each one take heed how he builds on it. For no other foundation can anyone lay than that which is laid, which is Jesus Christ. Now if anyone builds on this foundation with gold, silver, precious stones, wood, hay, straw, each one's work will become clear; for the Day will declare it, because it will be revealed by fire; and the fire will test each one's work, of what sort it is. If anyone's work which he has built on it endures, he will receive a reward. If anyone's work is burned,

> he will suffer loss; but he himself will be saved,
> yet so as through fire. (1 Cor. 3:5–15, NKJV)

In these passages, Paul refers to the bema judgment seat of Christ by using three illustrations. Paul refers to the judgment seat of Christ as building the foundation of salvation for Christ, being subject to searching judgment and being tested by fire. Paul uses resources such as gold, silver, precious stones, and etc. which means in the bema judgment seat of Christ, believers will be judged by their works and faithfulness. If they have been tried and been true to the ministry by building upon the foundation of Christ, they will receive a reward. In addition, Paul mentions wood, hay, and straw which means the deeds believers do that are not counted worthy of eternal recognition will be consumed by fire and turned into ashes (not going to hell, but God destroying unworthy deeds). The word *reward—misthós*—refers too wages, hire, and reward this means that when believers are judged, they will have rewards in the bema judgment.

In a reference scripture to the believers' judgment, Paul mentions something further in regards to the bema judgment. He mentions in

> Do you not know that those who run in a race all run, but one receives the prize? Run in such a way that you may obtain it. And everyone who competes for the prize is temperate in all things. Now they do it to obtain a perishable crown, but we for an imperishable crown. Therefore I run thus: not with uncertainty. Thus I fight: not as one who beats the air. But I discipline my body and bring it into subjection, lest, when I have preached to others, I myself should become disqualified. (1 Cor. 9:24–27, NKJV)

Paul states the believer's race is different from the race of competition. The race that occurs in the natural will result with one winner, but Paul states with certainty that all the believers will win. Paul uses the word *discipline* (KJV "keep under") *hupōpiázō*—the part of the face which is under the eyes, the face. Paul uses language that he will not allow anything under his eyes to prevent him from winning souls to Christ. He uses another metaphor: the word *disqualified* was used in athletic games. If a contestant failed to meet the basic training requirements, they could not participate at all; therefore, having any practical opportunity to win. Christians must take note that they are not competing with fellow Christians in this race because all will receive their prize! Christians are promised a crown that will not fade away. Christians should also be reminded not to judge other Christians' works because we—all who are saved—will appear at the judgment seat of Christ. The house of the Lord will be the home for those who believe in Him and when we appear at His judgment seat, we will be rewarded.

Dr. Tony Evans shares a story:

> In 1980, a young lady entered the Boston Marathon. She started the race looking great. And as the runners approached the finish line, she was leading the pack by a country mile, breaking all kinds of records. The crowd applauded as she crossed the finish line and was crowned champion.

> It was suspicious, however, that a woman who had never won a marathon before could win the Boston Marathon—especially by a country mile. Lo and behold, when they examined the situation, the girl started the race but then left the run and got on the subway, rode the subway for sixteen

miles, got off the subway, got back onto the route, and crossed the finish line first! When her cheating was discovered, she was, of course, disqualified from the race.

One thing for sure, you can't cheat your way into heaven; repentance of sin and confession of faith must be the prerequisites to go there! Shortcuts are not permitted nor necessary because one must repent. In fact, there's no Christological relationship without repentance of sin. Therefore, when we have heaven in view, we must take the necessary steps to get there. We must repent of our sins and aspire to keep a relevant relationship with the Shepherd. The ultimate goal of every believer should be entering into the eternal bliss of God and living in their eternal home with God forever. David has an extreme passion for giving God eternal worship. His worship will not cease in the house of the Lord, it shall continue. He passionately desires to have continued fellowship with God. We were made to worship God and our worship must not cease. It must continue as we transition from earth to heaven. We will give God glory for eternity and praise His name. God's desire for the sheep is to provide and protect and preserve His sheep despite their adversity. This is undoubtedly what "The Shepherd does for the Sheep—this allows David to have a personal testimony that he has learned that he does these specific things, He guides us, He guards us, and He guarantees us!"

REFERENCES:

Zodhiates, Spiros. *The Complete Word Study Old Testament.* Chattanooga: AMG Publishers, 1994.

Zodhiates, Spiros. *The Complete Word Study Dictionary New Testament.* Chattanooga: AMG Publishers, 1992.

Grudem, W.A. *Systematic Theology: An Introduction to Biblical Doctrine.* Leicester, England; Grand Rapids, MI: InterVarsity Press; Zondervan Pub. House.

Kendrick, K.M. "Sheep Senses, Social Cognition and Capacity for Consciousness." In *The Welfare of Sheep*, edited by Cathy Dwyer, 137. Netherlands: Springer Netherlands, 2008.

Calvin, John and James Anderson. *Commentary on the Book of Psalms.* Bellingham, Washington: Faithlife, 2010.

Dr. Jeremiah Wright (God's grace will never lead you where grace cannot sustain you)

Martin Luther - "This presence of the Lord is not to be perceived with the five senses; faith alone sees it, which is sure of the fact, that the Lord is nearer to us than our own-selves."

Matthews, Victor, Mark Chavalas, and John Walton. *The IVP Bible background commentary: Old Testament.* Illinois: IVP Academic, 2000.

Thomas, Robert L. *New American Standard Hebrew-Aramaic and Greek Dictionaries: Updated Edition.* Anaheim: Foundation Publications, Inc., 1998.

36. The Pulpit Commentary

Thomas, R. L. (1998). *New American Standard Hebrew-Aramaic and Greek dictionaries : updated edition.* Anaheim: Foundation Publications, Inc.

Robinson, Hadden W. "Trusting the Shepherd." Grand Rapids, Michigan: Discovery House, 2002.

Thomas, R.L. *New American Standard Hebrew-Aramaic and Greek Dictionaries: Updated Edition.* Anaheim: Foundation Publications, Inc., 1998.

The Preacher's Complete Homiletic Commentary: Watkinson, W. L. (1892). Psalm 1–25. In *Psalms 1–87* (Vol. 1, p. 113). New York; London; Toronto: Funk & Wagnalls Company.

W. A. VanGerman

MacArthur, John F. *The MacArthur Study Bible.* Nashville, TN: Word Pub, 1997. Electronic edition.

Evans, T. *Tony Evans' Book of Illustrations: Stories, Quotes, and Anecdotes from More Than 30 years of Preaching and Public Speaking.* Chicago, IL: Moody Publishers, 2009.

CPSIA information can be obtained
at www.ICGtesting.com
Printed in the USA
BVHW031638010320
573616BV00001B/5